The Digital Bind

STUDIES IN MOBILE COMMUNICATION

Studies in Mobile Communication focuses on the social consequences of mobile communication in society.

Series Editors

Rich Ling, *Nanyang Technological University, Singapore*
Gerard Goggin, *University of Sydney, Australia*
Leopoldina Fortunati, *Università di Udine, Italy*

Haunting Hands: Mobile Media Practices and Loss
Kathleen M. Cumiskey and Larissa Hjorth

A Village Goes Mobile: Telephony, Mediation, and Social Change in Rural India
Sirpa Tenhunen

Negotiating Control: Organizations and Mobile Communication
Keri K. Stephens

Cultural Economies of Locative Media
Rowan Wilken

Transcendent Parenting: Raising Children in the Digital Age
Sun Sun Lim

Shifting Dynamics of Contention in the Digital Age: Mobile Communication and Politics in China
Jun Liu

News in their Pockets: A Cross-City Comparative Study of Mobile News Consumption in Asia
Ran Wei and Ven-hwei Lo

(Im)mobile Homes: Family Life at a Distance in the Age of Mobile Media
Earvin Charles B. Cabalquinto

The Digital Bind: Constant Connectivity and the Reconfiguring of Family, Work, and Friendship
Jeffrey Boase

The Digital Bind

Constant Connectivity and the Reconfiguring of Family, Work, and Friendship

JEFFREY BOASE

OXFORD
UNIVERSITY PRESS

Oxford University Press is a department of the University of Oxford.
It furthers the University's objective of excellence in research, scholarship,
and education by publishing worldwide. Oxford is a registered trade mark of
Oxford University Press in the UK and in certain other countries.

Published in the United States of America by Oxford University Press
198 Madison Avenue, New York, NY 10016, United States of America.

© Oxford University Press 2025

All rights reserved. No part of this publication may be reproduced, stored in a retrieval system,
transmitted, used for text and data mining, or used for training artificial intelligence, in any form or
by any means, without the prior permission in writing of Oxford University Press, or as expressly
permitted by law, by licence or under terms agreed with the appropriate reprographics rights
organization. Inquiries concerning reproduction outside the scope of the above should be sent
to the Rights Department, Oxford University Press, at the address above.

You must not circulate this work in any other form
and you must impose this same condition on any acquirer.

CIP data is on file at the Library of Congress

ISBN 9780197798591
ISBN 9780197798607 (pbk.)

DOI: 10.1093/oso/9780197798591.001.0001

For my children, Nika and Keo

For my children, who are a kid.

CONTENTS

Acknowledgments   ix

Introduction   1

PART ONE   Connectivity in Context

1   The Social Implications of Constant Connectivity   9

2   The Configuration Approach   24

3   Social Configurations   49

4   Technological Configurations   74

PART TWO   Practices of Connection

5   Discovering Practices of Connection   95

6   Three Common Practices of Connection   113

7   At Work   134

8   With Family   153

9   With Friends   170

10   The Digital Bind   184

Appendix: The Promise and Perils of Digital Methods 190

Notes 195

Bibliography 199

Index 206

ACKNOWLEDGMENTS

The beginning of the COVID-19 pandemic occurred just weeks after I signed the publishing agreement for this manuscript. With two young children at home, I made their well-being my priority and put my writing on hold. During that time, I spent many hours sitting on park benches while they played, rereading work by Beck, Giddens, and Coser. Although I had little time to write productively, I was constantly thinking of how I might incorporate their ideas into this book. When my children finally returned to school two years later, I put these thoughts into writing. Between the fall of 2022 and the spring of 2023 I wrote the majority of this manuscript, with the final push necessitating that I work every weekend for a three-month block. And this brings me to my first acknowledgement: my children, Nika and Keo, to whom this book is dedicated. Their support and understanding as I spent many hours in my office was a gift. I am also grateful to Miki for keeping them active and happy as I toiled away. And I would like to thank my parents for their enduring support, and my mother especially for proofreading several drafts of this manuscript.

As this manuscript developed, I benefited from the feedback and encouragement of several colleagues. I am deeply grateful to Scott Campbell, Adriana de Souza e Silva, Rich Ling, Lee Humphreys, Bree McEwan, Tero Karppi, Julie Chen, Kate Maddalena, Hiu Fung Chung, Morgan Ross, Sarah Sharma, Colin Agur, Will Marler, Rhonda McEwen, and Jack Veugelers. I am also grateful to the reviewers for their helpful feedback. I received additional editing support and feedback on several chapters from Andrew/Aure Schrock of Indelible Voice. I was assisted in the data collection for this project by students working with me through the University of Toronto's Research Opportunities program, the Work Study program, and as hired research assistants. They include Jack Jamieson, Junji Zhi, Yingduo Tang, Weizhen Sheng, Paula Cho, junoh kimm, Jane Tran, Rayana Azar, Christine Kim, Vishal Monteiro, Yangbo Hu, Hirokazu Oda, Hai-Dao Le-Nguyen, Elizabeth Tong, Lela Elbarkoki, Marah Mufleh, Max Nyanin, Rayan Rahman, Grace Goldbaum, Kang Jag Wong, Maria Sillano, Natalie Chiovitti, Priya Vora, Rahma Saeed, Stefanus Welong, Giovanny Welong, Misha Gohar, Rida Saeed, Mariia Aresheva, Lauren Paul, and Dahye (Erica) Lee.

This book draws on research supported by the Social Sciences and Humanities Research Council of Canada and the University of Toronto.

INTRODUCTION

As mobile devices continue to evolve—from basic phones designed solely for calling to more sophisticated smartphones and wearable devices—what remains constant is that the portability of these devices creates new possibilities for social connectivity. By lowering our social dependence on place, mobiles open up the timing of our availability. They have enabled the technological reality of constant connectivity.

What has constant connectivity meant for social life? It is obvious that being more available for communication has the potential to impact how we connect with our family, friends, and coworkers. Since the diffusion of mobile phones and other wireless devices that enabled what James E. Katz and Mark Aakhus (2002) termed "perpetual contact," mobile communication scholars have studied the many ways in which constant connectivity has shaped and been shaped by social life. Yet a clear and straightforward answer to the question, What are the social implications of constant connectivity? remains elusive. The answer to this simple question is complex.

CONSTANT CONNECTIVITY IN CONTEXT

Constant connectivity has become part of life for much of the world's population. Between 2002 and 2022, the number of cellular subscriptions worldwide increased from approximately 1 billion to more than

The Digital Bind. Jeffrey Boase, Oxford University Press. © Oxford University Press (2025).
DOI: 10.1093/oso/9780197798591.003.0001

8 billion (Statista 2023), which is the same number of people estimated to be living on earth that year. Of the 8 billion mobile subscriptions in 2022, nearly 7 billion subscriptions included internet access, and this number is projected to steadily increase. Of course, some individuals and organizations have multiple subscriptions; it is clear that not every person alive in 2022 had a mobile subscription. Nevertheless, it is reasonable to infer from these numbers that much of the world's population had mobile access as of 2022, and that access will continue to grow.

Despite the widespread prevalence of mobile access, it is important to recognize that not everyone is equally connected. Although high-speed mobile infrastructure now blankets much of the earth, it has not reached all remote and economically disadvantaged regions. Moreover, although the cost of mobile devices and subscriptions continues to decrease, those who are most disadvantaged often cannot afford them, or they can only afford outdated devices and low-bandwidth subscriptions. Finally, a relatively small set of individuals choose not to own mobile devices or use them very infrequently.

Although connectivity is not experienced equally by all people in the world, the vast majority of those living today still have at least some minimal level of mobile connectivity. Those lacking data connections typically can still call and text through their mobile devices. Those with slow data connections can still use a variety of communication apps, albeit with lower-bandwidth audio and video experiences. This means that for most of the world's population, there is the technological possibility of communicating with others at any time.

Since the early days of mobile adoption and development, mobile scholars have studied the social implications of these devices. As I discuss in the next chapter, early studies of mobile use showed that mobile phones were mainly used to bond with close friends and family. It is tempting to attribute this pattern of connection to the nature of the devices themselves. Texting on these early devices required the cumbersome entering of messages through numeric keypads. Moreover, as these devices did not allow for the use of social media apps, knowledge of a specific phone number was necessary to initiate calls and texts. It seems reasonable to assume that these devices were used mainly to connect with close friends and family because the phone numbers of close individuals are more commonly known and because short messages are easier to manage with others who share contextual knowledge and understandings. In this account, the properties of technology itself can be used to explain a particular social outcome.

Although this technologically deterministic explanation holds appeal, it fails to capture the complexity of social life. While many studies found that individuals tended to use these devices with close friends and family, respondents in these studies tended to be adults living in economically prosperous countries. Other studies focusing instead on teens, or adults living in less prosperous countries, found that early mobile devices were often used to build new friendships and coordinate exchanges with weak social connections. In these populations, the benefits of connecting via mobile devices justified the effort of typing long messages on numeric keypads and getting phone numbers from people beyond their immediate social circles. This implies that while the design of these early devices may have influenced their use to some extent, their social implications have also been shaped by social context.

With the development of more complex mobile devices—particularly smartphones, which allow for the installation of social media apps and other communicative platforms—mobile scholars have continued to find that the social uses of these devices vary by a plethora of intersecting social factors. In many cases, they find that contemporary mobile devices are used to develop and maintain weak tie relationships. At the same time, they find that these devices are frequently used throughout the day to maintain close, bonding connections. In short, they show that as these devices have become more complex, so too are the myriad relationships that they are used to maintain and develop.

The finding that complex devices are used to maintain complex relationships in the context of constant connectivity is intriguing, but it poses a conundrum. How are we to make sense of these complex technical and social arrangements? Perhaps these arrangements are so complex that we are simply unable to provide a coherent and comprehensible explanation as to why they exist. While it may be tempting to simply conclude that such an understanding is not possible, we must at the same time acknowledge that while these patterns may be complex, they are not random.

In this book I argue that the social implications of constant connectivity exist in the form of communicative practices that occur within complex technological and social arrangements. In doing so, I provide three original contributions to our understanding of this topic.

1. A new theoretical framework called the *configuration approach.* This framework provides an understanding of how technological and social configurations contribute to the development of mediated communication practices.
2. An account of how technological and social configurations have become increasingly complex since industrialization.
3. A comprehensive empirical study that uncovers three common practices of connection used to navigate constant connectivity within complex social and technological configurations.

With this combination of theory, historic context, and empirical work, I offer a comprehensive account of the role that constant connectivity plays in social life.

OVERVIEW OF CHAPTERS

Chapter 1 reviews mobile communication studies focused on the social implications of constant connectivity. I use these studies to argue that the social implications of constant connectivity are influenced by both the design of mobile devices and the social situations in which they are used.

In Chapter 2, I develop a new theoretical framework called the configuration approach to make sense of the relationship between technological and social arrangements. The concept of "configuration" requires that we consider how both social and technological rules provide the conditions under which technologically-mediated social actions can occur. It is within these configurations that new practices of connection emerge, further embedding technology into social life.

Introduction

Chapters 3 and 4 discuss the development of contemporary social and technological configurations. I show that both social and technological configurations have become increasingly complex since industrialization.

Having made the case in Part I (Chapters 1 through 4) that the social implications of constant connectivity are shaped by complex social and technological configurations, Part II (Chapters 5 through 10) draws on an empirical study to explore communication practices that emerge within these complex configurations.

Chapter 5 outlines the multimethod study I designed to understand the practices of connection that have developed within the context of complex social and technological configurations. This study involves a unique data collection app that I designed to weave together a combination of digital trace, survey, and interview data.

Chapter 6 outlines three common practices of connection that I identify through the study. One such practice, which I call *media situatedness*, involves the reflexive choosing of media based on a variety of situational, relational, and personal considerations. I also find that individuals tend to have their many different kinds of relationships scattered across several apps, and even group interactions within apps. This *division of media* is the means by which individuals manage the complexity of juggling interactions across several different social institutions and relationships. Finally, I discuss how individuals collectively manage the potential of constant connectivity by creating *temporal boundaries*. These temporal boundaries typically involve the use of artifact-based media—often text messages and social media messages—so as not to interrupt their contacts' activities. Power in the form of communicative autonomy is critical to understanding how individuals implement these practices in their own lives.

Chapter 7 considers how these practices manifest within the context of work. I focus on practices within four kinds of occupations: knowledge, service, public sector, and goods production. The findings show that knowledge and service occupations often require that workers engage in media situatedness, maintain a division of media, and manage temporal boundaries. Workers in these occupations tend to have high levels of personal network complexity. In contrast, workers in public sector and goods-producing occupations are generally much more constrained in their ability to engage in these practices of connection.

Chapter 8 draws on the study results to examine practices of connection in the context of family, with a focus on partners and spouses, parents and children, supportive family relationships, and diverse family relationships. In all of these contexts, family members draw on technology in ways that strategically maintain temporal boundaries while still maintaining desired levels of interaction. Media situatedness was also observed in many kinds of family relationships, particularly with diverse family members, as text-based media were sometimes used to avoid conflicts that tended to arise in-person or by phone.

In Chapter 9 I explore the study results related to practices of connection within the context of friendship. I focus on friendships that are close, enduring, supportive, and diverse. I find that media situatedness is highly important because individuals often actively choose if and how they connect with their friends. Temporal boundaries are found to be important within all types of friendships, particularly with enduring friendships.

Chapter 10 concludes by considering how the results of this study show the various ways in which the digital bind manifests itself within the context of complex technological and social configurations. I discuss how practices of media situatedness and the division of media affirm and perpetuate personal network complexity. I also consider how temporal boundaries can help us to manage complex personal networks in the presence of constant connectivity. Taken together, I argue that these three practices of connection represent a binding of the digital into the social that is at the intersection of constant connectivity, social complexity, and technological complexity. I conclude by considering how this digital bind reconfigures social life and speculate about the future implications of the digital bind in regard to climate change and governance.

PART I

Connectivity in Context

The Social Implications of Constant Connectivity

This chapter draws on mobile communication research to examine the social implications of constant connectivity. Starting with early mobile studies at the turn of the century, I discuss the common finding that the connectivity enabled by mobiles leads to more intense communication with close friends and family. I then challenge the assumption that this type of mobile bonding has come at the expense of contact with weaker relationships. Drawing on other studies conducted throughout the world, I show that early mobile phones were also used to connect with weak tie relationships in specific populations. I then turn to more recent research, which indicates that smartphones are used to connect with a wide range of strong and weak relationships.

Taken as a whole, mobile studies show that the social implications of constant connectivity are not uniform but, rather, vary by the social and technological contexts in which they are used. I conclude by considering how this literature shows a tension between the technological and the social, whereby both mobile design and social circumstances influence, but do not determine, communication practices.

MOBILE BONDING

For many, the social implications of constant connectivity first manifested in the form of mobile bonding. Mobile bonding involves frequent

---

The Digital Bind. Jeffrey Boase, Oxford University Press. © Oxford University Press (2025).
DOI: 10.1093/oso/9780197798591.003.0002

and regular communication with close relationships via mobile devices, and scholars consistently found evidence of this phenomenon as mobile phones quickly became adopted in the 1990s and early 2000s. These early mobile studies found that mobile bonding manifested in several ways, and scholars described these various forms of mobile bonding in several influential writings. In this section, I will discuss the literature on mobile bonding by reviewing these influential writings and the empirical findings that underlie their development.[1]

Given that adoption of mobile phones and mobile texting diffused quickly and early in Japan, Japanese scholars were among the first to recognize this phenomenon, and their work has been highly influential in shaping our understanding of mobile use and its implications for social life. In particular, the edited volume *Personal, Portable, Pedestrian: Mobile Phones in Japanese Life* (Ito, Matsuda, and Okabe 2005), contained two papers that help to seed and popularize two conceptions of mobile bonding. One of these papers, by Misa Matsuda, drew on survey data from a variety of sources to show that mobile texting[2] and calling fosters what she calls *selective sociality*. Matsuda found that respondents identified their first- or second-most-often calling and texting partners as being spouses or romantic partners, friends in workplaces and schools, or friends at former workplaces or schools. She also found that the most popular use of mobile calling was to arrange meetings with friends and to inform family members of arrival times. Matsuda further used this data to show that call screening was a heavily used feature of mobile phones, which further speaks to their usefulness in allowing people to socialize selectively.

In another paper from this same edited volume, Ichiyo Habuchi (2005) developed an influential understanding of mobile bonding that he called *tele-cocooning*. Although tele-cocooning is a type of mobile bonding, it is conceptually different from selective sociality. Habuchi argued that tele-cocooning occurs when individuals use their mobiles to maintain contact with people that they rarely see in-person. Drawing on national survey data collected in Japan in late 2001, Habuchi found that 66% of mobile users maintain contact with "someone who I now rarely see in person but keep in good contact with via [mobile texting]" and that 46% of these users consider this person "irreplaceable and very important to me" (p. 178). Habuchi goes on to argue that tele-cocooning is driven by a sense of social insecurity and that maintaining familiar connections via mobile communication provides a way of coping with this insecurity.

Monadic clusters is another term that is evoked in discussions about mobile bonding, particularly in conversations about the impact of mobile use for political deliberations. Taking a theoretical approach, Kenneth J. Gergen coined this term when arguing that monadic clusters form because civil society is being, "slowly replaced by small, intensely interdependent communication clusters" (2008, 308). Gergen sees this as being the result of twentieth-century communication technologies, such as radio and TV, which decrease the need for public conversations about social and political issues. He also points to the development of transportation infrastructure as explaining why individuals are less rooted in their neighborhoods, again, decreasing local communal interactions. He goes on to theorize that "cell phone technology favors withdrawal from participation in face-to-face communal participation. Indeed, as many commentators demonstrate, public cell phone use invites antagonism and scorn. Simultaneously, however, the cell phone favors intense participation in small enclaves—typically of friends and family" (p. 302). While the concept of monadic clusters is somewhat similar to the concept of selective sociality, it differs by focusing on *clusters* of friends and family, rather than select individuals within family and work institutions.

Perhaps the most influential concept related to mobile bonding in the literature is that of Rich Ling's *bounded solidarity*. Ling developed this concept using a combination of social theory and empirical research. Ling finds empirical support for this concept in two coauthored research papers that use communication data gathered by a telecommunications company in Norway. In the paper titled "The Socio-demographics of Texting: An Analysis of Traffic Data" Ling and colleagues (2012) show that, on average, about half of the text messages that an individual sends and receives are with only five other persons. Moreover, about half of the calls an individual makes and receives are with only three other people. In another paper, titled "Small Circles: Mobile Telephony and the Cultivation of the Private Sphere" Ling and colleagues (2014) used the same type of log data to show that about two-thirds of calls and texts go to "strong ties" that are within a twenty-five-km radius. In this paper, "strong ties" are defined and ranked according to the total number of calls and texts occurring in the past three months. In short, both of these analyses indicate that in terms of texting and calling frequency, there is a large amount of mobile communication with a small number of geographically close individuals.

Ling provided an extensive and sophisticated explanation of these empirical findings in his book, *New Tech, New Ties: How Mobile Communication is Reshaping Social Cohesion* (2008). In this book he draws on social theory, qualitative interviews, and observations to argue that mobile phones have been woven into the everyday rituals that create modern-day solidarity. In Ling's words, "The assertion here is that these forms of ritual interaction are helping the peer group and the family to form cohesive bonds in ways that were not available in the recent past" (p. 186). Ling envisions that bounded solidarity is a type of cohesion that is somewhere between preindustrial societies in which individuals where constantly immersed in small and bounded groups of family and local community members, and the sort of individualism that theorists such as Scott Lash Ulrich Beck have argued is prevalent in contemporary societies. As Ling explains, mobiles have allowed for

a recalibration of how social cohesion is being worked out in society . . . while there is a tightening of the local group, it is not necessarily at the expense of involvement in the broader social flux of activities . . . . Rather than a quasi-corporate stop on the way to full individualism, perhaps we are dealing with the legacy of earlier, more communal forms of interaction. These are not as stiff as those defined by the church, the family, and tradition, but they still retain the human touch of social interaction that is a buffer against the other individualistic winds blowing in society. (pp. 186–187)

These concepts—selective sociability, tele-cocooning, monadic clusters, and bonded solidarity—have all played an important role in shaping our understanding of mobile phones and their social implications.

Additionally, two related concepts have been influential in explaining how mobile bonding occurs in everyday life.

Christian Licoppe's concept *'connected' presence* refers to perception of being present with distant others through the use of mobile devices (Licoppe 2004). Licoppe argued that, compared to calling, mobile texting was particularly conducive to maintaining a sense of 'connected' presence, since it allows for continual light-weight interaction throughout the day. Drawing on empirical studies conducted in France, Licoppe found that 'connected' presence happened mostly between close friends and family. While the concept of 'connected' presence is not directly about interaction with close relationships, it provides a way of understanding how mobile bonding occurs.

Another important concept that explains the mechanisms of mobile bonding is that of *microcoordination* and *hypercoordination*. Rich Ling and Brigitte Yttri developed these concepts through a series of group interviews conducted in Norway (Ling and Yttri 2002). They use the term microcoordination to refer to situations in which individuals use their mobiles to change the times or locations of in-person meetings. Hypercoordination includes microcoordination but adds emotional and social communication that occurs through mobile devices, as well as the ways that mobile devices are used in acts of self-presentation. Self-presentation would include the status that individuals find in particular types or brands of devices, how these devices may be decorated, and the places in which they are used. Although micro- and hypercoordination are not directly about bonding communication with close friends and family, Ling and others have used these concepts when explaining how mobile devices are used in these types of close relationships.

BEYOND MOBILE BONDING: ABANDONING THE ZERO-SUM PERSPECTIVE

On the surface, selective sociability, tele-cocooning, monadic clusters, and bonded solidarity and the related concepts of 'connected' presence and micro- and hypercoordination all point to the role that mobile phones play in supporting strong relationships. However, when we look more closely at the evidence and specific definitions of these terms, a more complicated picture emerges. Selective sociability is about mobile communication with specific individuals in work and family institutions. Tele-cocooning is about mobile communication with undefined close relationships that are not often seen in-person. Monadic clusters are thought to be bounded groups of like-minded friends and family, and bounded solidarity focuses on frequent communication with geographically close relationships. Although these concepts all involve mobile use within strong relationships, are they really about the same conceptual thing?

Mobile scholar Scott Campbell has argued that in addition to focusing on different dimensions of strong relationships, all of these concepts imply that mobile bonding comes at the expense of engagement with a broader set of community ties. He dubs this phenomenon "network privatism" and draws on my work with Tetsuro Kobayashi and colleagues (2014; 2015) to argue that network privatism implies a zero-sum perspective. Under this perspective, it is assumed that additional communication with existing strong relationships comes at the expense of interaction with new and weaker relationships. The reasoning here is that people have a limited amount of time for social interaction, and therefore interaction with strong relationships comes at the expense of interaction with weaker relationships.

The zero-sum perspective appears not only in mobile communication studies but also in technology studies more broadly (Boase 2008; Boase and Wellman 2006). It is flawed in its assumption that social interaction with one kind of relationship must always come at the expense of social interaction with another kind of relationship. There are many nonsocial activities that we do during the day—such as watching videos, sleeping, and so forth—and we can do less of these asocial activities if we spend more time texting, calling, and using social media. Moreover, because mobile devices are always typically small and potentially with us, we can use them while carrying out nonsocial activities, such as waiting in line or during commutes. Given the range of social and nonsocial activities that people do throughout the day, it is possible that interaction occurring through mobile phones and other technologies is displacing or changing the nature of nonsocial activities, not interaction with weaker relationships.

If we abandon the zero-sum perspective, we do not necessarily abandon the idea that mobile devices can play an important role in the communication that occurs in our inner circle of friends and family. Communication frequency is an important dimension of relational closeness (Granovetter 1983; Marsden 1987), and communication is generally higher with strong relationships than with weaker relationships. In general, people interact with their weak ties less often than their strong ties, so it is reasonable to expect that mobile communication would also be less frequent with weak ties than strong ties. Moreover, it's still possible that mobile phones play an important role in reconnecting with dormant weak tie relationships. Mobile calls, texts, and more recently, audio messages, locations shared, social media posts, and so on, may serve an important role in "getting back in touch" and "touching base" with weaker relationships, even though, overall, these moments of reconnection would be few and far between for any given weak tie relationship (Boase et al. 2015; Kobayashi et al. 2015).

All of this points to the possibility that the role of mobile devices in strong relationships would simply be more apparent, since people spend more time connecting with these types of relationships than their weaker relationships. To some extent, these findings might also be the result of a bias during surveys and interviews toward recalling interactions with people who are most frequently and regularly seen in-person (Brewer 2000). Regardless of the reason, less frequent mobile contact does not imply that mobile phones are unimportant for maintaining contact with weak ties. Abandoning the zero-sum perspective opens the possibility that mobile technology can also play an important role in developing and maintaining a diverse array of relationships. In fact, despite the attention given to mobile bonding throughout the literature, research has consistently found different ways in which mobiles are used outside of strong tie relationships.

THE SOCIAL SHAPING OF MOBILE USE: EARLY FINDINGS

Frequent mobile communication with strong ties drove early adoption and incentivized telecommunication industries to invest in mobile infrastructures. This rapid and widespread adoption helped to widely establish expectations of constant connectivity in the form of mobile bonding. However, empirical research has shown that even in the early stages of adoption, mobile phones also played a role in the development and maintenance of weak ties and other kinds of relationships.

In this section, I will first discuss how a few early mobile studies linked mobile use to weak tie development among teens in Japan and showed a much wider range of uses in less economically developed countries. These countries provide an important contrast to work done primarily in North America and Europe, and they help to broaden our understanding of how these early mobile phones were used differently in different social contexts. Drawing on this research, I will then consider the relationship between social circumstance and technological possibilities.

Teens living in Japan during the early 2000s occupied a somewhat atypical set of social and technological circumstances. Unlike teens in many other countries, teens in Japan live highly scheduled lives. Nearly all junior and senior high school students participate in after-school activities such as "cram school" and sports clubs (Onoda and Omi 2023) and they have often been observed returning home late in the evening. Japan's telecommunication infrastructure was unusually advanced in the early 2000s, and many teens had their own phones that could send and receive text messages. Messages were entered through numeric keypads; however, these keypads were optimized for entering Japanese characters, and extensive messages could be written at a reasonable speed.

In a 2006 study of 501 high school students living in Tokyo, Tetsuro Kobayashi and I found that the more teens texted, the more they reported texting with both strong and weak relationships (Boase and Kobayashi 2008). Among the heavy texters, there was the perception that mobile phones were helping them to both strengthen strong relationships and to develop weaker relationships. Drawing on literature from psychology and social network analysis, we theorized that although teens clearly want to maintain close friendships, they are also at a time in their lives when they want to explore their social worlds by developing new relationships. Mobile texting can help with both social pursuits, as it enables teens to maintain a 'connected' presence and at the same time nurture new relationships while they are busy with school and extracurricular activities. In short, the social limitations of Japanese teen life, the desire for social exploration, and the unique technological features of early Japanese mobile phones created a situation that was conducive to using mobile phones to develop weak relationships.

In his extensive literature review about the social implications of mobile phones, Wilken (2009) makes the case that studies in South Africa and Tanzania (Goodman 2005), the Philippines (Pertierra 2009), and Jamaica (Horst and Miller 2006) all show how mobiles can be used to develop new relationships within particular social and cultural contexts. In these studies, routine development of weaker and diverse relationships is more directly linked to economic exchange. In his words, "...mobile communications have been taken up and adapted to form yet another way of ameliorating the effects of poverty (or the threat of it). In these examples, individual actors have developed a variety of complex network strategies involving mobile phones that maximize their (potential) access to the widest possible pool of social capital resources" (Wilken 2009, 144).

In another review of more than 200 studies focusing on mobile use in economically disadvantaged countries, Jonathan Donner (2008) finds more mixed social implications of mobile use. On the one hand, he finds some studies that clearly show how mobiles are used by small enterprises, farmers, and the self-employed in ways that help them develop their businesses and generate income. At the same time, other studies indicate that mobile phones are still used for social purposes in these contexts as a tool to maintain contact with friends and family. Nevertheless, even in these cases, the social uses of mobile devices are clearly different from the type of mobile bonding found in economically advantaged countries. For example, given that the cost of calling is often calculated based on the duration of calls, individuals have developed "beeping" practices, whereby they will not answer calls and instead interpret the ringing as having a particular meaning (Donner 2007). For example, without answering, a parent may know that their child needs their assistance, or a regular client of a taxi driver needs to be picked up. Regardless as to whether mobiles are being used for financial transactions or more social purposes, few individuals can afford to use them for the type of frequent, strong tie exchanges that define mobile bonding in economically prosperous countries.

While the technical capabilities of mobile phones in poorer countries were quite limited at the time of this research, individuals still found ways of using them for the purposes of exchange and direct transactions. For example, Jenna Burrell's (2010) study of mobile phone use in Uganda showed how individuals share their phones for various purposes, and often in ways that are related to gender dynamics. In some cases, women were gifted phones by their husbands, and they then allowed others to use their phones for a small fee as a means of generating income. In other cases, men may offer their phones to women in attempts to lure them into relationships. This research shows a pattern of mobile use that is very different from the type of mobile bonding found in more economically prosperous countries, where individuals can afford their own devices and the costs of using them frequently. Moreover, it shows how social dynamics—in this case, gender differences and lack of financial resources—shape mobile use.

The development of weak ties, entrepreneurial activities, and phone sharing practices in various populations throughout the world during the early stages of mobile phone diffusion show patterns of usage that are clearly different from mobile bonding. They show that mobile use is shaped by social and financial circumstances.

SMARTPHONES: NEW SOCIAL OPPORTUNITIES

Smartphones expanded opportunities for interaction from only calling and texting to a range of new messaging and social media apps. Additionally, the presence of higher-speed internet connections, along with

The Social Implications of Constant Connectivity

processing, storage, and high-resolution cameras, further increased the opportunities to utilize these new apps for exchanging photos and videos and to engage in synchronous video calling. What has remained unchanged from nonsmartphones, however, is the fact that these devices continue to provide the potential for constant connectivity. In other words, while the devices and range of possible communications changed with the diffusion of smartphones, the potential for constant connectivity has remained. What have the expanded technical opportunities provided by smartphones meant for social relationships?

The studies reviewed in the previous section show that even when mobile phones are limited to calling and sometimes texting, they can be used to foster new and weaker relationships in particular situations. It is fair, however, to argue that phones limited to calling and texting may provide fewer opportunities for the development of new and weaker relationships than smartphones. When used for social purposes—as opposed to calling businesses, for example—calling and texting require that individuals have the phone number of the person they are contacting. Phone numbers can be considered personal information, and thus acquiring someone's phone number often requires some basic level of trust and perhaps familiarity. In the case of teenagers in Japan or people in countries where economic exchanges require the development of new relationships, it's reasonable to expect that people may be more open with their phone numbers than people who have little interest or need to develop large personal networks of new and weak relationships.

In contrast to phones that are limited to calling and texting, smartphones provide access to social media platforms that people can use to easily "friend" or "follow" others whom they have never met personally or only know minimally. Keith Hampton has argued that regularly using social media over time can provide persistent contact with and passive awareness of others and their lives (Hampton 2016). In this way, smartphones may be particularly valuable for the development of new and weak relationships by providing people with a sense of awareness about these relationships as they use them to view social media feeds throughout the day. At the same time, persistent contact and passive awareness can serve to further strengthen already strong relationships by providing an additional layer of information about the activities and emotional states of these individuals.

Social media messaging apps may further enable weak tie maintenance and development. This may have been especially true during the period when smartphones first diffused. During this time, smartphones often lacked the ability to partake in group text messages through the older SMS systems. This was not the case with many social media messaging apps, such as WhatsApp and WeChat, which enabled group chats even in their earliest versions. Group chat functionality can be used to maintain and develop communication with sets of individuals, many of whom may be weak ties. Unlike one-to-one exchanges through text messages, group chats may be more likely to involve indirectly known individuals, such friends of friends. This is because group chats can be initiated by one individual who creates the group, and members of that group need not know the phone numbers or other contact information of the others in order to be included.

In addition to providing constant access to social media platforms, smartphones can also be used to find events, businesses, and other locations where people have the opportunity to meet others in-person. Map apps are particularly useful in this regard because they provide real-time information about location-specific activities. Lee Humphreys (2007) studied the use of one such app, Dodgeball, through a series of in-depth interviews held in several major US cities. Dodgeball was an early example of an app that allowed people to share their locations with a set of friends, and much like popular social media platforms, users were able to create friends without the use of phone numbers or other personal information. Humphreys found that people used this app to meet with a core group of close friends as well as less-well-known friends. This finding fits with the insights about location-aware mobile media provided by Daniel Sutko and Adriana de Souza e Silva (2011). They argue that the use of location-aware social media can result in a strengthening of existing relationships when the identities of users are known and woven into these types of apps. At the same time, they argue that these apps

The Social Implications of Constant Connectivity

can foster interactions with new and diverse others when they conceal the identities of the users.

While smartphones provide more opportunities for building and maintaining large networks of weak relationships than previous phones that were limited to calling and texting, it is critical that we not repeat the zero-sum fallacy; increased communication with weak ties need not come at the expense of communication with stronger-tie relationships. In addition to the opportunities that social media apps provide to expand and maintain people's social horizons, these same apps can also be used in ways that strengthen already strong core networks. The added layer of connection that these apps provide means that users may have an even greater awareness of those that they already see frequently and those to whom they already feel close. Moreover, the messaging apps offered through social media platforms can be used for small group–based conversations with close friends and family. These conversations can further add an additional layer of communication onto the already frequent communication that may be happening in-person or by phone. Moreover, just as the map apps and other location services can help people meet up with weak ties, they can in the same way facilitate in-person interaction with stronger ties.

In short, smartphones provide a new set of opportunities by virtue of the fact that they have become wireless computers. The rise of smartphones has coincided with the development of wireless internet infrastructure and social network platforms, and this has opened up a new range of possibilities for maintaining and developing a variety of relationships, near and far. In this way, the opportunities that smartphones provide are tethered to platforms that are constantly changing, in both their design and popularity. Thus, mobile phones are no longer self-contained blocks of hardware that have clearly understood and unchanging technological functions—that is, voice calling and texting. Their constant connectivity and the ability to install new software apps means that their ever-changing technical possibilities give rise to new and ever-changing social possibilities.

CONCLUSION

The social implications of constant connectivity have varied considerably as mobile devices have evolved and been adopted by different populations. Adults in economically prosperous countries primarily used early mobile phones to bond with strong tie relationships. These devices were often used to selectively connect with and maintain a 'connected' presence with close friends and family throughout the day. However, early mobile research also showed that in different populations throughout the world, these same devices were used to maintain and develop weaker relationships. The expanded technological capabilities of smartphones created more opportunities to connect with weak tie relationships, while at the same time providing additional options for communicating with stronger ties.

In short, while there is some evidence to suggest that the technological capabilities of mobile devices influence their social use, there is no evidence to support the view that specific social implications necessarily flow from these technical capabilities. When individuals are in social circumstances that motivate them to connect with others—as was the case with teenagers in Japan leading highly scheduled lives and entrepreneurs in economically disadvantaged countries—they find ways to deal with technological constraints. This points to the diverse ways mobile communication practices emerge within particular social and technological arrangements.

In the introduction to this book I asked, What are the social implications of constant connectivity? The literature reviewed in this chapter shows that there is no simple answer to this question because constant connectivity alone does not determine particular social outcomes. Rather, the social practices that emerge under the precondition of constant connectivity vary depending on particular social and technological arrangements. Individuals develop communication practices that fit within these varied circumstances and the technological possibilities that their devices provide. Within certain combinations of social and technological arrangements, individuals may develop mobile communication practices that favor strong tie connections. In other combinations, they may develop practices that help to develop weaker relationships. In yet other combinations, they may use mobile devices to communicate with a mix of strong and weak ties.

While it is clear that mobile practices are influenced by both social and technological arrangements, the literature reviewed in this chapter does not provide any further understanding of exactly how this influence operates. If we are to understand the social implications of constant connectivity, we require a framework that can help us unpack the salient aspects of social and technological arrangements and their influence on mobile communication practices. This framework should help us to understand how and why communication practices emerge in the presence of constant connectivity. The development of such a framework is the focus of the next chapter.

2

The Configuration Approach

The mobile communication studies reviewed in the previous chapter indicate that the social implications of constant connectivity vary by the design of mobile devices and by social circumstances. While these studies provide us with ample empirical evidence to suggest that both technological and social factors influence mobile use, they do not help us to understand exactly how this influence occurs. To make sense of these empirical findings, we require a theoretical framework. In this chapter, I review two useful theoretical perspectives and use them to develop a new theoretical approach.

I first discuss how the social affordance approach helps us to understand the role of technological design on mobile communication practices. I argue that while this approach is useful in explaining how technology can enable and constrain certain communication practices, it does not provide a framework for understanding the role that social environments play in the development of mobile communication practices. I then discuss how a social ecological framework helps us to understand the influence of social environments on technological adoption and use but fails to fully articulate the role of technological design. Having reviewed these two approaches, I then propose a new approach that orients us to consider how both technological design and social environments provide sets of opportunities and constraints in which individuals reflexively develop communication practices. This approach extends Anthony Giddens's (1984) theory of structuration by applying it to nonhuman actors. I call this the *configuration approach*.

The Digital Bind. Jeffrey Boase, Oxford University Press. © Oxford University Press (2025).
DOI: 10.1093/oso/9780197798591.003.0003

SOCIAL AFFORDANCE

The social affordance approach highlights the role of perceptions of technology in the adoption and use of technology, while acknowledging the materiality of technological design. In this way, it avoids simplistic accounts of technology adoption and use that focus only on subjective understanding or material design. The social affordance approach is a branch of a more general psychological approach called "affordance theory," which was developed by psychologist James J. Gibson to understand how animals perceive and navigate their environments. In Gibson's definition, "the affordance of anything is a specific combination of the properties of its substance and its surfaces taken with references to an animal" (1977). Gibson's definition transcends the objective/subjective dualism, in that the objective properties of the objects are significant only in relation to an animal's subjective perception of them. This implies that the same object can have multiple affordances perceived by different types of animals. For example, a tree might be perceived by a bird as a place to perch, and at the same time be perceived as a source of shade by a lion. In Gibson's words,

> Although an affordance consists of physical properties taken with reference to a certain animal it does not depend on that animal.... An affordance is not what we call a "subjective" quality of a thing. But neither is it what we call an "objective" property of a thing if by that we mean that a physical object has no reference to any animal. An affordance cuts across the dichotomy of subjective-objective and helps us to understand its inadequacy. (Gibson 1977, p. 69)

Those working in computer science were among the first to apply the concept of affordance to the relationship between technological design and human perception. Don Norman explains, "An affordance is a relationship between the properties of an object and the capabilities of the agent that determine just how the object could possibly be used" (2013, 11). Norman advocates for a "user-centered design" approach in which designers consider the tasks of users. In this approach, designers include signifiers that help users understand how technologies can be used to carry out tasks.

Communication scholars apply the term "social affordance" even more narrowly to describe social uses and perceptions of technology. For example, Fox and McEwan (2017) developed a scale of perceived affordances across different media, such as texting, email, and social media. Their measure captures perceived affordances that are inherently social. For example, their measure captures the extent to which different communication technologies can help people feel the presence of another person during an interaction ("social presence"), the ability to convey emotion ("bandwidth"), and how easy it is to get a message to someone ("accessibility"). Drawing on a range of mobile scholarship, Andrew Schrock (2015) developed a typology of affordances that apply solely to mobile media: portability, availability, locatability, and multimediality.

Communication scholars have been criticized for focusing almost exclusively on the perception of affordances and neglecting the material realities of technological design. For example, social media algorithms can influence social media use even when they are not being perceived by users (Nagy and Neff 2015). While this criticism has merit, it is important to consider that studies such as Fox and McEwan's are not intended to capture all aspects of affordances. However, it is also fair to recognize the material role that technology plays in communication processes. For my purposes, I find it useful to consider the relationship between the material/design side of communication technologies and their perceived affordances.

Returning to mobile use, let's start by considering the role that design played in early texting practices. Texting with early mobile phones required entering messages through cumbersome numeric keypads. Inputting a single letter or character often required hitting the same button several times or a combination of buttons. This material reality of early mobile phone design created a situation in which short messages took significantly less time and effort to write than longer messages. The design of early mobile phones explains the common finding that individuals tended to text mainly with close friends and family. Given that close

The Configuration Approach 27

friends and family share a great deal of common knowledge, short messages are typically sufficient for basic tasks such as coordinating daily activities or maintaining a sense of connection throughout the day. In contrast, weaker connections tend to lack the context necessary to understand short messages. In short, the time- and effort-intensive nature of writing keypad-based messages on early mobile phones explains why they were often used to communicate with close social ties.

While this technologically deterministic explanation helps us make sense of early mobile use with close friends and family, it was later contradicted; teens in Japan used these same devices to connect with and build networks of *weaker* relationships. A purely technological explanation is also contradicted by studies showing that individuals living in economically disadvantaged countries used mobile media to connect with weaker relationships for business purposes. It is difficult to reconcile these diverse social uses of the same technology by only considering the design of the technology. If it were the case that design alone explained usage, we would expect to find uniform social uses of early mobile phones, regardless of the population using them.

Considering the perceived affordances of early mobile phones helps reconcile these device findings. Returning to Fox and McEwan's (2017) typology of perceived affordances, sending messages through early mobile texting would generally be considered low bandwidth, since keypad entry limited message length. Meanwhile, texting would generally be considered high accessibility, since early texting still allowed individuals to send messages directly to others, regardless of their concurrent activities. When considering these two perceived affordances, the use of mobile texting in close relationships still makes sense. The low bandwidth of keypad texting implies that messages might often be so brief that they are difficult to understand without the context known by close friends and family. It's also likely that the accessibility of texting would lend itself to contacting close relationships throughout the day, regardless of their activities.

The perceived affordance of accessibility also explains why early mobile phones were used to send text messages to weaker relationships in certain populations. Teens in Japan had highly structured lives with few other opportunities to interact with new and weaker relationships during the day. The perceived accessibility of mobile texting made it a clear choice for connecting with these relationships. Mobile calling would not be an option, given that teens in Japan spend much of their waking lives engaged in uninterruptible activities, like schooling. Their daily activities would also prevent them from using computer-based email, and social media did not exist at the time. Although the low bandwidth of keypad-based texting still presented a challenge, teens in Japan pioneered the development of abbreviations and text-based emoticons to compensate for the lower bandwidth of texting (Okada 2005).

Although the social affordance approach helps reconcile different social uses of early mobile phones, its focus on design and perception means that the social world is not given any systematic, theoretical attention. The opportunities (and constraints) of technology are the only factors that the approach considers outside of an individual's subjective understanding of technology. To be fair, the affordance approach does allow for individual researchers to "fill in" social factors as they are perceived by individuals. However, such backfilling is done at the researchers' discretion, leading to a lack of systematic focus. Therefore, it has been difficult to accumulate knowledge about how the opportunities and constraints created by social circumstances influence the adoption and use of mobile technologies.

Returning to the example of teens in Japan using keypad-based texting, the social affordance approach allowed me to refer to the structured nature of teen life. However, it did not provide a systematic way of thinking about structure. Nor did it help produce a broader theoretical account of how social structure can influence mobile use or perceptions of affordances. In this way, the social affordance approach treats material design only as an external condition necessary to consider in relation to perceived affordances. It fails to recognize that it is necessary to consider social structure's relation to perceived affordances. In short, the social affordance approach only gives us part of the story. It helps us to understand the role that technology and perceptions of technology play in social life. However, by focusing on technology and perception, little systematic attention is given to the role of social factors in the adoption and use of these technologies. To better

understand the social factors that provide opportunities and constraints for mediated communication, I will now turn to social ecology
theory.

SOCIAL ECOLOGY

Social ecology theory has been used in different ways by scholars working in diverse fields. While the term "ecology" broadly refers to the
relationship between organisms and their environments, Stokols (1996)
explains that social ecology "gives greater attention to the social, institutional, and cultural contexts of people-environment relations" (p. 285).
Social ecology was not specifically developed to explain the social factors that influence technology adoption and use. However, scholars have
adapted the ecological approach in this way. For example, John Dimmick's (2002) "theory of the niche" provides an understanding of how
new media compete and coexist with more established media. Dimmick originally developed this theory to explain how mass media such
as newspapers and television compete for attention and has since used
it in collaborative research to consider how interpersonal communication media such as the telephone, instant messaging, and email (Ramirez
et al. 2008; Dimmick et al. 2000) compete for usage within personal networks. The social ecology approach has more recently been applied to
understand how individuals navigate multiple social media platforms
(Zhao et al. 2016; Boczkowski et al. 2018).

More directly related to our interest in constant connectivity, Rich
Ling draws on social ecology theory to explain the widespread adoption of mobile phones. In his book *Taken for Grantedness* (2012), Ling
explains, "As a device goes through the diffusion process, it is possible
to see the 'space' that it moves into as an empty or open niche . . . . As
it moves into a niche, it can out-compete other previously established
technologies and reform the boundaries of the niche" (pp. 31–32). To
illustrate how this theory can be used for our purposes, I will discuss
how Ling applies this concept to explain the rise of mobile calling and
texting. His argument is that such uses fill a niche created by the social
uses of landline phones, automobiles, and clocks.

Landline phones may have allowed for voice-based interaction over distances, but a great deal of social interaction still occurred in-person. In industrialized societies, interaction was scheduled through social practices that relied on mechanical timekeeping. Providing a rich historical account that draws on germinal work by Lewis Mumford (2010) and Eviatar Zerubavel (1985), Ling shows how the industrial revolution's demand evolved mechanical timekeeping from fitting into the social niche of routine life in monasteries to being a central means of coordinating work. In this way, the clock found its foothold within a relatively small but influential group and eventually displaced earlier forms of coordination in society.

Ling also traced how the diffusion of the automobile influenced the development of urban and suburban life, to the point that it became the default transportation system in many societies. The car freed individuals from the time constraints embedded within public transportation systems. However, it had the unintended consequence of producing a system in which public transportation became less available. As with the clock, Ling tells a story of how a technology gained a foothold within an existing set of practices and eventually became so embedded into social practices that its use became "taken for granted." Ling establishes how the clock and car gained footholds within specific niches and eventually moved into a social ecosystem in which they became the dominant technologies for coordination in many societies.

Ling then discusses how mobile phones fit within a niche that these two technologies created. Namely, relying only on clocks and cars limited opportunities for individuals to change existing travel arrangements. Once a meeting was scheduled, there was little opportunity to adjust it while in transit. Mobile phones could occupy this niche by offering a way to change plans, adding new flexibility to interactions, which Ling and Yttri (2002) called "microcoordination" in an earlier work. As Ling sums up,

> this challenges (or perhaps modifies) time as a technology of coordination. When there was no mobile-based communication, agreeing on a time along with a place was a nearly absolute coordination

strategy. Mobile communication pushes aside time in a regime of transportation coordination, at least within the small group. The mobile phone also changes car-based logistics, since it challenges (or perhaps supplements) time-oriented coordination, especially for smaller groups. The mobile phone allows iterative planning through the use of calls, texts, and, for some, social networking sites. (2012, 186)

Ling concludes his book by referring to his previous research collaborations, in which mobile phone data were used to show that frequent contact occurs with a small set of geographically proximate people (Ling et al. 2014; Ling, Bertel, and Sundsøy 2012). He argues that mobile-enabled microcoordination has allowed for the rise of what he calls the "digital gemeinschaft." The word *gemeinschaft* is a reference to Ferdinand Tönnies' concept of how preindustrial communities entailed frequent contact with like-minded others. Ling argues that by filling the communication niche between the car and clock, mobile phones helped people maintain the intimate sphere of friends and family, despite larger social changes that instead pulled us toward isolation or individualism.

The social ecology approach provides a compelling way to understand the diffusion of new technologies. Rather than presenting technology as an external force that simply imposes its logic onto social life, social ecology helps us to see how existing social practices contain "spaces" (niches) that new technologies can "move in." As technologies become more embedded into daily life through diffusion, they can slowly encroach on the use of previously dominant technologies. In the case of the mobile phone, its use has mostly displaced the use of telephone booths in many countries, and increasingly, it is displacing landline phones as well. However, the adoption of one technology need not necessitate that another technology becomes obsolete; clocks and cars remain part of society.

Another important contribution of the social ecology approach is its recognition that people often combine multiple technologies to carry out social actions. As I have advocated previously (Boase 2008), considering how several technologies are combined provides context for understanding their social significance. For example, if we were to study mobile calling in isolation, we might find that mobile-calling colleagues about work-related matters is often conflictual in nature. This clash may lead us to conclude that mobile calling lends itself to negative interactions between colleagues. However, if we considered the relationship between email and mobile calling in the same setting, we might find that mobile calling is used to resolve occasional misunderstandings that arise during email exchanges. In other words, the synchronous nature of calling allows individuals to more easily work through misunderstandings than asynchronous emailing. In this way, occasional calling fills the niche of resolving misunderstandings in asynchronous text-based media. Without it, misunderstandings would fester and escalate.

The social ecological approach provides a way of formally understanding how the social world influences the adoption and use of communication technologies. While Rich Ling uses this approach to understand mobile adoption, it can also be used to explain technological adoption and use within subpopulations. Returning to the example of keypad-based mobile texting, a social ecological approach draws attention to social constraints placed on Japanese teens in the early 2000s. Social constraints created a situation in which in-person interaction with peers typically occurred in highly structured environments—schools, cram schools, and clubs—where opportunities for relational development were minimal. These social constraints created a niche in which teens used keypad-based communication to develop new, weaker relationships in short periods of travel time. Keypad-based entry was generally more cumbersome than in-person communication for developing these types of relationships. However, its adoption makes sense within an institutionally constrained set of interactions.

Recognizing the dynamic nature of social practices allowed social ecology scholars to understand the adoption of new technologies up to the point where they were so prevalent and part of daily routines that they were "taken for granted" (Ling 2012). Additionally, a social ecological approach helps us understand communication technologies even after they reach a steady state of adoption and usage. As Ling's argument implies, the temporally rigid practices of scheduling appointments for specific times and traveling to them existed for several decades. It was the steady-state nature of these practices that created a niche that was eventually filled by the mobile phone, which in turn led these practices to become more temporally flexible. Thus, while my tracing of Ling's arguments focuses on mobile adoption, social ecology is also useful for understanding why individuals consistently use certain technologies over long periods of time. Once a technology has become embedded into widely held social practices, these practices are likely to remain constant until a new technology is introduced that better fills certain gaps.

The social ecological model has an advantage over the social affordance approach. It draws attention to the role that social practice plays in the adoption and steady state use of communication technologies. This attention is missing from the social affordance approach, which brackets the social world to mainly focus on individual perceptions of technology and its material properties. However, the social ecological approach alone does not provide the theoretical focus on material properties of technologies or individual perceptions of those properties. In order to address these shortcomings, I propose a new approach that draws on elements of the social ecological and affordance approaches.

THE CONFIGURATION APPROACH

I have developed what I am calling "the configuration approach" to provide a framework for understanding the social implications of technology use. This framework draws attention to both social and technological configurations. This approach also acknowledges the roles of human and technological agency. It expands Anthony Giddens structuration theory to include the structure and agency of technology.[1] To unpack the components of this theoretical approach, I will define and discuss each of them in turn.

Social configurations are social structures, which Giddens (1984) defines as rules and resources involved in reoccurring social actions. Giddens argues that rules can be explicit—for example, when a workplace forbids employees from making personal calls during work hours—or tacit, such when an employee knows that using their phones to make personal calls during work hours would be considered inappropriate. He defines resources as control over material objects and goods. An example of a resource would be a phone that can be used to carry out actions, such as calling friends, texting family, and navigating to new locations.

Human agency occurs as individuals take specific social actions. Following Gidden's structuration theory, agency and structure are often two sides of the same coin; individuals take social actions that draw on rules and resources, and in doing so their actions can reproduce social structure. However, not all social actions will necessarily reproduce social structure, which is important to consider both when explaining social actions that violate social rules and when examining the emergence of new social practices. New social practices are often required when technologies are introduced and social rules surrounding their use have not been established. If these new practices are successful, then they may be repeated and eventually become new social configurations.

For example, when mobile phones started to diffuse throughout the population and workers started taking them to the office, there was a lack of rules regarding their use. One can imagine that office workers in those early days may have sometimes failed to silence their devices and decided to engage in personal calls in front of their colleagues. In traditional office environments these disruptions would have likely resulted in stern warnings and the development of new rules forbidding the personal use of mobiles during work hours. Workers then acting in accordance with these new rules would be adopting and reproducing new social configurations.

Human reflexivity is the process that stands between social configurations and human agency, through which individuals make sense of their social contexts and plan future actions. Giddens conceived of reflexivity "not merely as 'self-consciousness' but as the monitored character of the ongoing flow of social life" (Giddens 1984, 3). While Giddens considers reflexivity to be part of agency, theorist Margaret S. Archer (2012) instead argues that it stands between the structure/agency dualism. Archer also identifies four types of reflexivity: communicative, autonomous, meta, and fractured. She argues that communicative reflexivity involves internal conversations that need to be completed by others. In contrast, autonomous reflexivity involves self-contained internal conversations that directly lead to action. Metareflexivity includes inner conversations that are critical about previous inner dialogues, while fractured reflexivity is internal conversation that does not lead to action and intensifies individual distress.

Archer's approach to reflexivity provides a useful framework for thinking about the process by which individuals think about technology in social action. Rather than treating all individuals as going through a similar process of "technology use," it can help us to understand several different approaches and outcomes. For example, when deciding if one should text, call, social media message, or email a new acquaintance, someone who relies on communicative reflexivity might confer with a friend to determine the most appropriate method. In contrast, an individual taking an autonomous reflexive approach would consider what they know about that individual and the perceived affordances of each technology before deciding. Someone else engaged in metareflexivity might critically consider the various approaches to thinking about the appropriate use and eventually decide on a method without a strong sense that it is ideal. Finally, those experiencing fractured reflexivity would be unable to determine which technology to use and decide not to contact this new acquaintance at all.

While reflexivity is sometimes considered to be the antithesis to habit, Archer argues that they do not exist in a zero-sum relationship. Archer does not deny the existence of unconscious habitual behaviors, but rather, she argues that these behaviors are less common in contemporary societies in which individuals must navigate a wide variety of social configurations. By the same token, she argues that habitual action tends to exist when social configurations are constant throughout time, as habitual action tends to reproduce existing configurations.

In the context of mobile use, we can consider various ways in which mobile use can involve a mixture of habit and reflexivity. For example, the tendency for individuals to unconsciously glance at their mobiles throughout the day is a habit shared by many. Nevertheless, within different situations, individuals may make reflexive decisions about how, when, or weather to respond to new notifications that they see when glancing at their mobiles. They might also make decisions about removing their mobiles from sight as a means of avoiding disruption to certain activities. These reflexive decisions may then lead to new habits, that require less attention over time. In fact, there is already empirical work examining mobile usage that shows that individuals often show a mix of conscious and less conscious mobile use (Bayer et al. 2016).

Another example highlighting how reflexivity can lead to habit is as follows. When an individual starts a new job, they may be told that there are informal rules in their office that limit the use of mobile phones for personal reasons. At the same time, this individual may feel that it is important to respond immediately to text messages from their spouse, as this communication behavior has become critical to the coordination of their daily activities. Given these competing social configurations, the individual may reflexively decide that while at the office, they will only respond to messages from their spouse and ignore messages from anyone else. Over several days or perhaps months, they form a habitual response of completely ignoring all messages except for those from their spouse.

In this example, Archer's theory would point us to the initial conditions that required that the individual reflect on their mobile use: the starting of a new job. Here, the immersion of the individual into new social configurations required that they reflexively choose how to act, and as the individual remained in that same consistent situation, their chosen actions became habitual. It is only with the changing of that situation—such as perhaps the introduction of a new rule completely restricting all mobile use at the office—that this individual would then need to stop all mobile phone use at work. They may break their previous habit of texting their spouse by reflexively deciding to put their phone out of sight at the start of each workday. Eventually, this new behavior would likely become habitual.

To sum up, reflexivity is how individuals determine which actions to perform. It stands between social configurations (i.e., structure) and human agency. Individuals engage in a reflexive process of choosing new actions as new configurations and situations arise. If these actions are repeated because the social configurations surrounding them remain constant, they may eventually become habitual. However, once these social configurations change, these habitual actions will be disrupted, and individuals will again reflexively choose their future actions.

Technological configurations are the properties of technology that enable technical action. Like social configurations, technological configurations consist of rules and resources that control hardware and software. Rules can take the form of software protocols, algorithms, or scripts, while electricity is a necessary resource for running digital technologies. Hardware is also configured such that it follows rules. For example, when the device is turned off, pushing a mobile phone's "on button" sets off a series of intended events within the device. This series of events unfolds in a particular way due to hardware configurations within the device.

Technological agency occurs when technology takes specific actions. Although it is common to think of technology as passive, its agency becomes more obvious when it fails to function as expected. For example, communication within an entire organization is thrown out of balance by a virus. Yet even when technology functions as expected, it still performs actions. These actions can be as simple as the ringing of a phone or as complicated as the processes social media platforms perform when determining what posts should appear in an individual's feed.

Recognizing that nonhuman entities have agency is common in science and technology studies. Bruno Latour developed this ontology as part of his actor-network theory (ANT), which broadened the meaning of agency to include nonhuman entities that lack intentionality and free will (Sayes 2014). Nonhuman agency permits the causal significance of technology in social actions. In discussing the causality of nonhumans, Latour argues, "There might exist many metaphysical shades between full causality and sheer inexistence: things might authorize, allow, *afford*, encourage, permit, suggest, influence, block, render possible, forbid, and so on" (2004, 226, italics added). Treating technology as having agency because it affords social actions that could not have happened otherwise squares nicely with the affordance approach.

RECURRING MEDIATED COMMUNICATION PRACTICES

Structuration theory conceives of agency and structure as two sides of the same coin. Actors draw on their understandings of explicit and implicit social rules while also reflexively monitoring the flow of social activities. To the extent that they act in ways consistent with these rules, they reaffirm them through their actions. Of course, not all actors will always follow rules, and social structure changes when new practices lead to the development and adoption of new rules. Paying attention to the reflexive process can help explain why particular actors are more likely to follow rules than other actors. It can also help us understand how actors develop tacit or explicit rules, particularly when provided with new options for communication as new technologies emerge.

In the configuration approach, a similar process is envisioned with technology. Rules are central to technological design, and they exist in the form of software scripts, protocols, algorithms, and arrangements of physical components. As technologies carry out their processes in any given moment, they act according to those rules. Like humans, technologies do not always follow rules, such as when they break down or are co-opted by other sets of rules in the form of viruses. While there is no evidence that technology currently possesses reflexivity, it is possible that artificial intelligence eventually will possess reflexivity. In any case, it is not necessary to assume that technology possesses reflexivity to acknowledge that, like humans, the agency and structure dualism also exists as technologies enact given rules.

Having applied the structure and agency dualism to technology, we can now better conceive of the relationship between technology and social action. Rather than viewing technology as directly impacting social action as an external force, it is possible to view technological action as existing in a relationship with social action. To the extent that technology is used regularly within recurring communications—what I refer to as *practices of connection*—there will tend to be a symbiotic relationship between the social and technical configurations that is simultaneously enacted by both humans and technology. See Table 2.1 for an overview of the key concepts used in this approach.

For example, consider the common practice of texting someone before an in-person meeting to slightly alter its time or location. This type of "microcoordination" (Ling and Yttri 2002) has become a common social practice in many societies. From the lens of the configuration approach, microcoordination fuses technical and social configurations that require the agency of humans and technology. The practice requires mobile devices that are configured to send and receive short messages, and notifications to alert users in the form of chimes, haptic vibrations, or on-screen notifications when messages are received. These technical configurations create the possibility of microcoordination. At the same time, microcoordination also requires human social configurations in the form of rules. Humans need to comprehend that it is appropriate

Table 2.1. KEY CONCEPTS OF THE CONFIGURATION APPROACH

	Technology	Human
Configuration	Rules and resources embedded into hardware and software that influence how technology acts.	Rules and resources that influence how humans act. Rules include both tacit and explicit understandings of appropriate actions.
Reflexivity	No evidence at this time. Future AI systems may possess reflexivity.	The mental process through which humans monitor and consider social actions.
Agency	Technological action that occurs through the running of hardware and software.	Human action.
Practices of connection	Recurring communicative actions in which both humans and technologies exercise agency while drawing on social and technological configurations.	

to notify someone they are planning to meet if they are running late or want to meet in a slightly different location. This sense of appropriateness is essentially a widely shared implicit rule. It requires the shared understanding that when two people meet in-person, close to the meeting time it is appropriate that both individuals have their mobile devices handy.

The configuration approach explains why mediated communication practices tend to be robust, even when individuals fail to follow them in particular instances. Returning to the previous example, it is true that someone may choose to ignore the convention of texting to let a friend know that they are running late. However, this breach of etiquette could result in relational damage or conflict, lowering the chance of such a breach occurring again. In cases when etiquette is breached without repercussion, there is likely an unequal power dynamic between the individuals involved that supersedes the implicit rules surrounding the interaction. These power dynamics too are social configurations—the result of unequally distributed rules and resources. In the case when a manager fails to text a subordinate with the information that he is running late to a meeting, the implicit rule—that the subordinate should not mention this breach of etiquette—supersedes the etiquette itself. In short, mediated communication practices tend to be robust to the extent that they are congruent with social configurations.

Technological configurations also tend to be robust when they are embedded into established mediated communication practices. The widespread adoption and use of certain technological configurations into social life incentivizes producers to maintain core functionality. For example, the basic functionality of telephone calls is that an individual enters a unique identifier, traditionally in the form of a phone number, and the device linked to the identifier produces a ring or other notification. This basic functionality has not changed much in the past century. Given that this general type of configuration has been widely integrated into social practices throughout the world for decades, there is little reason for companies to drastically change how phone functionality works. While it is true that certain mobile apps have replicated

The Configuration Approach

this functionality within a constellation of other communicative configurations (e.g., in addition to texting and voice messages), the basic configuration remains. If telecommunication providers or technology companies were to completely remove this basic functionality, the social disruption would be tremendous. In other words, changing technological configurations that have already been deeply embedded into social practices would disrupt social configurations that depend on them. While such disruptions are not completely out of the realm of possibility, the larger point is that established mediated communication practices tend to reinforce both social and technological configurations. These mediated communication practices also change over time, particularly as new technological or social configurations are introduced into the system. However, in general, the more deeply embedded mediated communication practices are within the larger frame of social and technological configurations surrounding them, the more robust they tend to be. In this way, social and technological configurations tend to align, to the extent that they are consistent with longstanding and widely spread behaviors.

In short, both human and technological configurations must align for mediated communication practices to endure. The configuration approach helps us to be aware of and articulate these configurations as a way of explaining recurring mediated communication practices. Moreover, the configuration approach acknowledges the role of both human and technological agency in how potential configurations are utilized in specific practices. In any given situation, the individuals involved must reflexively decide to follow these social rules through specific actions. Moreover, the specific technology must act according to its configurations, as without this technological agency, mediated communication practices could not occur.

Just as the configuration approach helps us understand reoccurring mediated communication practices, it can also explain why new technologies are adapted into social practices. In this approach, new hardware and software can be understood as providing new technical configurations that may potentially fit within a niche of existing practices.

In this way, the configuration approach formalizes certain aspects of the social ecological approach.

SOCIAL ECOLOGY AND THE CONFIGURATION APPROACH

Ling applies the social ecological approach to understanding the adoption of mobile phones, drawing our attention to the role of technologically mediated practices and how they provide niches within which new technologies can be adopted. Over time, widespread adoption, driven by the emergence of new mediated communication practices, can displace or modify previously established mediated communication practices. The configuration approach provides a conceptual formalization of this process by providing us with a language to identify various aspects of this process as it relates to technological and social configurations. Moreover, the configuration approach also provides a way of understanding the relationship between the social and the technical within established social systems.

It is important to keep in mind that although an ecological approach implies that there is an "evolution," it does not imply that technology and society are evolving in a single direction that is getting progressively better. While some people may have this association, it is important to keep in mind that changes are not always for the best and that change may occur in very different ways across different populations. In other words, the social ecological approach only implies that there tend to be niches within mediated practices that leave open room for new practices to emerge. These changes occur in complex ways, depending on the differing practices that occur between different social contexts.

The configuration approach points to the congruence in technological adoption between technological configurations and social configurations. As discussed earlier, technological configurations refer to material designs—hardware and software arrangements, rules, or scripts—that enable technological devices and systems to carry out regular and predictable actions. Likewise, social configurations refer to explicit and implicit rules, which often take the form of cultural understandings or deeply embedded schema. As new technologies become available, they may be more likely to be adopted if they fit within the logic of existing social configurations.

Returning to Ling's discussion of mobile phone use, the technical configurations provided by portable network-connected devices fit within the existing need to connect with others during emergencies and for microcoordination. In this example it is tempting to see social configurations as more critical to the adoption of mobile phones than the technological configurations. However, if the technological configurations of portability and constant network connectivity did not exist, it would be impossible for new mediated communication practices of microcoordination to emerge. Social and technological configurations need to exist in congruent ways for the mediated communication practices that lead to mass mobile adoption and use to emerge.

SOCIAL AFFORDANCE AND THE CONFIGURATION APPROACH

Under the configuration framework, social affordances still exist as the relationship between perceptions of what technologies allow and the material reality of how those technologies function in practice. However, this approach further draws attention to technological affordances, which exist as the relationship between perceptions of what social structure allows and the reality of what social structures actually allow in practice. Put differently, just as technology provides opportunities for social actions, social structure also provides opportunities for social actions. Actors must reflexively perceive both what the technologies can allow them to do and what social structure allows them to do.

As an example, perhaps at the end of the workday I discover that the subway I usually take home is experiencing delays. I may wish to get in touch with a colleague in a nearby building to ask if he could give me a ride home. If I were only to consider the most effective way to reach this person, I might determine that a phone call would be the best way to quickly get his attention. However, this would be a mistake, as I know that this friend works in an office where personal calls are frowned upon. The social rules at his work would not allow for this type of communication, and breaking these rules might cause friction between us. Reflexive awareness of the social structure in which my friend was embedded would instead lead me to text my friend. Even though it might not get his attention as effectively as a phone call, it would be more likely to get his attention than alternatives such as an email or social media message. In this situation, I would be reflexively aware of the social affordances of the technological configurations available to me and also aware of the technological affordances of my friend's social configurations at work. Ultimately, my choice of medium would be influenced by the affordances of both the technological and the social.

The configuration approach diverges from social affordance theory in that it further draws attention to how individuals reflect on the rules and resources available to them for social actions. Thus, within the realm of reflexivity, perceived technological affordances are given equal theoretical weight as perceived social configurations. By including both how technologies can be used, and the social rules and resources related to that use, the configuration approach allows researchers to formalize and understand perceptions of both the social and the technical. The recognition and systematic attention paid to rules and resources then helps move our understanding of mediated communication practices beyond a purely psychological bracketing of social structure and toward a conception of these practices that helps us understand the role that technology plays within larger social systems. It allows for the systematic understanding of broader mediated communication patterns by referring to distinct combinations of social and technical configurations.

REVISITING MOBILE STUDIES

In the previous chapter I reviewed literature about the social implications of constant connectivity. In this section I consider how the configuration approach helps us to make sense of these findings.

As discussed, the configuration approach leads us to consider how technical and social configurations both provide opportunities and constraints within which individuals develop communication practices. Applying this approach to early mobile studies reviewed in the previous chapter, we can see why scholars found that adults in economically developed countries used early mobiles to call and text close friends and family. In terms of technical configurations, the configuration approach leads us to consider factors such as the weight/portability of early mobiles, the fact that these devices were optimized for calling, and the requirement that users must enter phone numbers in order to communicate with others. In terms of social configurations, this approach would further lead us to consider factors such as the tacit rules that frequent and empathic communication is part of close relationships and that individuals should arrive on time to in-person meetings unless they communicate otherwise. Taking these technological and social configurations into account, we can see how reflexive individuals would conclude that calling was useful for staying in touch with strong relationships throughout the day and for microcoordinating interactions with these relationships. The configurations of these early mobile devices were optimal for frequent communication and coordination with stronger relationships. In contrast, there is less need to frequently communicate with weaker relationships and a lower chance of knowing their phone numbers.

The configuration approach can also be used to explain why teens in Japan used mobile texting to develop new weak tie relationships. The technical configurations of these early devices in Japan were limited to calling and texting, but the social configurations of this population were significantly different than those of adults. Rules at school and clubs limited opportunities for informally developing new relationships, despite providing students with opportunities to meet new peers. However, there were no rules forbidding texting while commuting or during other times of day when moving between school and after-school activities (Ito 2005). When considering these social constraints and the short intervals available for relational development, the material portability of these devices became more salient than the limits of keypad-based text entry. Teens in these circumstances found ways of coping with the limitations of keypad-based texting. Through the actions of these individuals and their devices, mobile texting for the development of weaker relationships became commonplace in this population.

The configuration approach further helps to explain why those living in economically disadvantaged countries used early mobile devices differently from those in economically prosperous countries. Those in poor countries could not afford frequent communication or justify frequent communication for social purposes. Nevertheless, early mobiles still allowed entrepreneurs and small business owners opportunities to carry out business-related transactions, and they developed practices of SIM sharing and other ways of lowering costs as a means of carrying out these vital exchanges. In other words, people found ways to use these devices outside of their intended designs because the social configurations in which they are embedded made such strategies worthwhile. These unintended uses imply that early adopters applied reflexive thinking as a means of creatively working around technological limitations.

Finally, the more current literature regarding the social implications of smartphones found that individuals use these devices for a wide range of practices. The configuration approach leads us to consider that smartphones allow for a wider range of communicative actions than early mobile phones. This creates new opportunities for connecting with strong and weak ties. This approach also leads to the expectation that individuals in social configurations that encourage strong tie connection would tend to use smartphones for connecting with these types of relationships. By the same token, it leads us to expect that individuals in configurations that encourage the formation and development of weaker ties will tend to use smartphones for these purposes. This further implies that individuals need to be reflexively aware of the many types of relationships that they wish to maintain or develop and then draw on the variety of communication apps available to them as a means of accomplishing these relational demands. In the remainder of the book, I will further explore the nature of these social and technical configurations and the practices of connection that individuals develop to navigate them.

CONCLUSION

The configuration approach provides a conceptual framework that can be used to understand the adoption and incorporation of technology into social life. It pays equal attention to social and technical configurations, social and technical agency, and the role of human reflexivity (and perhaps someday with the development of AI, technological reflexivity). By giving equal causal weight to humans and technology, it avoids simplistic understandings that place all causal weight on one side of the equation. Rather, the configuration approach cues us to pay attention to both social and technological configurations and to consider how these structural factors create contexts in which reflexive individuals develop practices of connection.

Returning to my initial question about what constant connectivity means for social life, the configuration approach helps us to understand constant connectivity as a condition under which practices of connection can be reflexively developed. When developing these practices, individuals are limited and enabled through social and technological configurations. As these configurations vary, so too will practices of connection vary in the presence of constant connectivity.

The configuration approach further helps to explain how certain practices of connection may become dominant within common technological and social configurations, even though any given individual will reflexively engage in a variety of practices. The configuration approach leads us to theorize that practices of connection will go through a type of selection process. In this process, practices that are most congruent with common social and technological configurations will typically become adopted by large sets of individuals. Conversely, practices that "bump up" against common social or technological configurations will tend not to be repeated or adopted on a mass scale. This means that while there is likely a lot of variation in how individuals reflexively understand and develop their practices of connection, practices that are repeated and adopted within broader populations over time will tend to be consistent with the common social and technological configurations of those populations.

Understanding the broad social implications of constant connectivity at a population level ultimately requires an understanding of how common practices of connection fit within common social and technological configurations. The next two chapters will focus on common social and technological configurations, while Part II will focus on common practices of connection that exist within the context of these configurations.

3

Social Configurations

As argued in the previous chapter, the configuration approach implies that constant connectivity allows individuals to develop mediated practices of connection that fit within social and technological configurations. Under this theoretical framework, the social implications of constant connectivity can be understood as the practices of connection that draw on and perpetuate social and technological configurations, thereby tightening the digital bind. The configuration approach further leads us to expect that while individuals may reflexively choose to enact a wide variety of practices, those practices that are most congruent with commonly occurring social and technological configurations will tend to be adopted by the population at large. This means that understanding the broad social implications of constant connectivity necessarily entails understanding commonly occurring social and technological configurations.

What are the commonly occurring social and technological configurations that enable and constrain practices of connection? In this chapter, I will address the first part of this question by drawing on sociological literature to discuss contemporary social configurations that constrain and enable practices of connection. I argue that personal network complexity is a prevalent contemporary social configuration that includes three dimensions: institutional complexity, relational complexity, and temporal complexity. I trace the development of personal network complexity from the time of industrialization to the present.

The Digital Bind. Jeffrey Boase, Oxford University Press. © Oxford University Press (2025).
DOI: 10.1093/oso/9780197798591.003.0004

SOCIAL SIMPLICITY AND PREINDUSTRIAL LIFE: AN IMAGINED PAST

Sociology has been deeply influenced by theories about the social impact of industrialization. Despite the many differences between the writings of influential sociologists such as Karl Marx, Max Weber, and Emile Durkheim, they all share a concern with how the development of large urban, industrial centers changed social life. They also prefer to explain the social changes caused by industrialization, rather than deeply exploring what life was like beforehand. Preindustrial social life was often compared with industrial life, rather than being the focus of sustained study.

One of the most influential works on preindustrial social life was *Community and Society* (1957), first published in 1887 by Ferdinand Tönnies. In *Community and Society* Tönnies argues that preindustrial *gemeinschaft* communities were held together by common bonds of kinship, locality, and friendship. He argues that these bonds of blood, place, and mind dominated relationships in the rural villages that were the homes of most people living in preindustrialized societies. While there were differences between these three types of relationships, all three tended to be intimate and rely on cooperation via shared customs, values, tacit knowledge, and beliefs. Tönnies presents an imaginary of past communities where people lived in harmonious, emotionally close relationships with like-minded others.

In contrast to *gemeinschaft* societies, Tönnies argues that industrialized *gesellschaft* societies "superficially resemble the gemeinschaft in so far as the individuals live and dwell together peacefully. However, in the gemeinschaft they remain essentially united in spite of all separating factors, whereas in the gesellschaft they are essentially separated in spite of all united factors" (1957, 64–65). The separation Tönnies refers to is emotional detachment and a lack of common understanding, and he argues that relationships have become primarily based on rational calculation in industrialized societies.

Tönnies' theory relies on assertion rather than evidence. Like other influential works of its time, it is undeniably Eurocentric and based

Social Configurations

on outdated understandings of "natural" relationships.[1] However, this book remains relevant insofar as its imagined description of preindustrial relationships has rooted itself into the contemporary popular imagination writ large. Regardless of whether Tönnies' theory measures up to historic reality, we have retained this imagined contrast between the cozy rural communities of the past and the harsh city life of the present day.

THE ROOTS OF SOCIAL COMPLEXITY

The industrial revolution brought new opportunities for interaction and relational development. Agrarian life typically required that individuals live and work with their extended families in multigenerational homes nested in small, rural communities. Spending most waking hours with other family members severely constrained opportunities to develop other kinds of relationships. Given limited transportation infrastructure and time-intensive farming practices, interactions outside the family were further limited to local communities. While there also were nomadic groups, the bulk of preindustrial agrarian relationships were restricted to kin and local ties.

The development of urban centers, rail systems, and factories all increased opportunities for interactions and relationships outside the family. Factory work required that individuals spend most waking hours working alongside others outside of the home. Rail systems facilitated the movement of people from geographically and culturally isolated rural locations to urban centers. Urban life therefore required interacting with unfamiliar others. Influential sociologists such as Emily Durkheim, Karl Marx, Max Weber, and Georg Simmel all grappled with the impact of these structural changes on the individual. They all focused on the psychological implications of everyday interactions with strangers and those known in only limited capacities for instrumental ends. For Durkheim, the result of this urban shift was "anomie"; Simmel proposed that it led to a "blasé attitude." Weber argued that it was part of a rational frame that built an "iron cage," while Marx saw urban life as merely alienation stemming from exploitive relationships. What unifies these theorists is the weight they place on the psychological impact of interacting with others for specific ends. Unlike rural residents, urbanites lacked relational history, shared experience, emotional closeness, common social norms, and mutual understandings. These features of modern relationships—all of which revolved around a lack of shared understanding and limited interactions—were thought to typify industrial social life.

These understandings of industrial social life imply a connection between social complexity at the "macro" societal level and relationships at the "micro" individual level. At the macro level, the division of labor brought through urbanization created a complex social organization. Factory work, migration to urban centers, and the development of complex urban and transportation infrastructures necessary to facilitate the flow of goods and people created a division of labor that Durkheim referred to as "organic society." In organic society, different sets of individuals contribute to the creation and delivery of goods and services. Labor becomes more specialized, as do the relationships involved in that labor.

This macrolevel social complexity resulted in microlevel social complexity in daily life. The division of labor required that individuals inhabit multiple social positions throughout their waking hours. For example, a husband within a family setting becomes a stranger within an urban setting while commuting to work and a laborer within the factory where he works. Thus, in a single day, this individual must inhabit multiple roles in relation to the individuals with whom he is interacting, each of which requires different types of behaviors. While it is true that individuals also had multiple roles in preindustrial settings, the switching between these roles would have been less frequent, given that individuals often worked with their family. In short, the societal complexity created by the increasing division of labor intensified personal network complexity for individuals, in terms of who they interacted with daily, and the social roles they played during those interactions.

ROLE COMPLEXITY

My use of the term "complexity" is not intended to signal my use of complexity theory, although my argument about the nature of complexity may be consistent with some aspects of this approach. Complexity theory pertains to entire dynamic systems, while my interests lie more in the social and technological configurations in which individuals are embedded. While I do look for consistent patterns across sets of individuals, it is beyond the scope of my argument to determine how these patterns manifest at a system level. Rather, my approach to social complexity draws on the work of sociologist Rose Laub Coser.

In the book *In Defense of Modernity: Role Complexity and Individual Autonomy* (1991), Coser offers a convincing and useful way to understand social complexity in everyday life. Drawing on Coser's theory, I will discuss how the development of industrialization provided conditions for the lived experience of social complexity. As industrialization increased, large, complex industrial and governmental organizations flourished. These organizations included public and private corporations and bureaucracies, such as companies, hospitals, and educational institutes. These organizations offered many "middle occupations" in which a considerable portion of employees were neither at the very bottom nor the top of the organizational hierarchy. In the case of the United States, Canada, Japan, and many European countries, late industrialization endured throughout most of the twentieth century. Because these middle occupations existed in large and stable organizations, they tended to be stable and provide individuals with jobs that often lasted the duration of their careers. This stability provided the conditions in which the duties and expectations of workers were clearly defined and well known to others. Workers coordinated activities through these stable and clearly defined roles that allowed for the large-scale production of goods and services.

Coser draws extensively on Robert K. Merton's role theory to understand the implications of middle occupations for daily social life. According to Merton, social roles entail sets of social expectations tied to an individual's position within social institutions such as work and family.[2] Within a single role, an individual may interact with a variety of others, and they must adjust their behavior accordingly. For example, a teacher is expected to behave differently when interacting with students than when interacting with parents, other teachers, their principal, or administrative staff. While a teacher is still a teacher when interacting with these different types of people, the expectations and norms of interaction vary considerably. Thus, a single role can have a set of expectations or interactional norms that require a teacher to adjust their thoughts and behavior. Social complexity in daily life becomes more evident when considering that individuals often move between several role sets during any given day.

Coser (1991) argues that less complex role sets in preindustrialized societies limited individual autonomy. "In groups that offer complete security, in which roles partners hardly change, and in which mutual expectations remain stable, there is relatively little opportunity to innovate or weigh alternatives of thought and behavior. A gemeinschaft is such a group" (71). Drawing on Lewis Coser's (1974) notion of "greedy institutions" —those that demand total commitment from their members—she makes the case that the greedy nature of *gemeinschaft* society limits individual autonomy by only providing simple role sets. Here, the unit of product is the family, which means that the same family members must live and work together for much of their waking life. In this common scenario, roles are well defined, and each family member had little opportunity to make decisions that deviate from their expected roles or to consider their own personhood separate from them.

Coser argues that social complexity in daily life is a hallmark of modernity. In the remainder of this chapter, I will first discuss the shift toward service- and knowledge-based economies that has occurred since the time of Coser's writing and then consider the implications of this societal transition for the rise of personal network complexity.

Social Configurations 55

PERSONAL NETWORK COMPLEXITY

Much of Coser's work was developed in the 1960–1980s United States as the country was transitioning to a more service- and knowledge-focused economy. Although Coser does not explicitly discuss the implications of this transition in her theory of role complexity, she clearly distinguishes between early industrialization and the type of industrialization occurring at the time of her writing. She acknowledges that the type of factory work common to early industrialization typically required only limited role sets. The rise of professions enabled the increased autonomy that she sees as a hallmark of modernity. In this section, I will specifically focus on the social implications of service- and knowledge-based occupations for what I call *personal network complexity*.

Daniel Bell popularized the notion that there has been a shift toward more service- and knowledge-oriented industries in his book, *The Coming of Post-Industrial Society* (1973). He argues that in preindustrial societies, life is a "game against nature" whereby uncontrollable natural events, such as seasonal temperature fluctuations and droughts, determine economic life. In contrast, life in industrial society was a "game against fabricated nature . . . . The machine predominates and the rhythms of life are mechanically paced: time is chronological, methodological, and evening spaced" (126). Finally, he typifies postindustrial service economy societies as being

> a game between persons. What counts is not raw muscle power, or energy, but information. The central person is the professional, for [they are] equipped, by [their] education and training, to provide the kinds of skills which are in increasingly in demand in the post-industrial society. If an industrial society is defined by the quality of goods as marking a standard of living, the post-industrial society is defined by the quality of life as measured by the services and amenities—health, education, recreation, and the arts—which are now deemed desirable and possible for everyone. (127)

Bell attempts to capture the economic and cultural shifts that typify postindustrial societies. While the statement "services and amenities... now deemed desirable and possible for everyone" glosses over deeply rooted inequalities, it nevertheless represents an ideological view that pervades postindustrialized societies. This idea that "everyone"—not just those of privileged groups—ought to have the opportunity to access services and amenities implies an individualistic orientation.

Individualism has a broad intellectual history that spans philosophical, political, economic, and sociological theory. I will focus on Urlich Beck's individualization thesis, which is one of the most influential and compelling sociological accounts of this change as it relates to service- and knowledge-based economies. Beck argues that the decline of stable, long-term work and family arrangements in these economies drove individualization. He identifies the labor market as the "motor" of individualization. While industrialized society centered on class identities that resulted from lifelong socialization and participation in labor, service and knowledge labor markets do not require this long-term approach to specific kinds of work. For example, in an industrially based economy, a boy raised by parents working on a factory line would typically be socialized to see himself as coming from this "kind" of family, trained to expect that he will have this type of job when he grows up and then work in this type of job for his adult life. In contrast, a child raised in a service- and knowledge-based economy may not necessarily be socialized to identify with his parents' jobs, nor would they necessarily assume that they will have the same type of job as an adult.

The downsizing of large organizations during and since the time of Beck's writing in the 1980s and 1990s has only increased the precarious employment that drives individualization. Downsizing has led to the flattening of hierarchies within large organizations, and short-term contract-based labor has become common. Increased "flexibility" at the organizational level made employment more precarious. As of 2020 in the United States, the median length of time that wage and salary workers stayed at their current employer was 4.1 years (Bureau of Labor Statistics 2020). The median was longest for those working in management (5.8 years), legal (5.8 years), architecture and engineering (5.1 years), and education (5.0). It was shortest for workers in service occupations (2.9 years).

Beck argues that new social mobility brought about by the more regular changing of jobs and careers has meant that education defines how individuals navigated a competitive labor market. Workers were often learning new skills and bodies of knowledge to work in different positions. They may also have worked in several different types of organizations in their lifetimes, each time "learning the ropes" about explicit and implicit expectations of their roles. This orientation toward constant learning is particularly true for those working in highly skilled, well-paying positions.

Beck also considers the implications of changes to family life for individualism. Over the life course, family life became increasingly complex in service and knowledge economies. Individuals were typically married or cohabitated multiple times throughout their lives, and the proportion of people living in unique configurations has been steadily on the rise. According to a US-based study conducted by the Population Reference Bureau (Vanorman and Jacobsen 2020), the percentage of households consisting of married couples with children decreased from 44% to 19% between 1960 and 2017. During the same period the percentage of single-parent households more than doubled (from 4% to 9%) and the percentage of households containing only one person increased (from 13% to 28%). Similar trends have been found in Canada, where household size has been decreasing and single-person households have been rapidly increasing (Milan 2015).

The decline of nuclear families, the prevalence of alternative family arrangements, and the increasing number of adults living alone is the result of many developments occurring since the middle of the twentieth century. Divorce is now commonplace, people are generally getting married later, or not at all, couples tend to have fewer or no children, individuals are more likely to be married multiple times, common-law marriages have increased, and same-sex marriages have become legal in many countries and are increasingly common. Additionally, young adult children often live with parents, children more often move between multiple homes as part of a weekly routine, more families have stepchildren and -parents, and more people are living alone. These societal shifts have changed the composition of families and households, and within an individual's lifetime they will likely experience several family arrangements (Pew Research Center 2015).

These broad changes in family and household composition have coincided with a broadening of expectations and norms surrounding family life. Using data from several surveys conducted between the late 1950s until the 1980s, Thornton (1989) finds a "weakening of the normative imperative to marry, to remain married, to have children, to restrict intimate relationships to marriage, and to maintain separate roles for males and females" (873). Revisiting this topic with data from the 1980s and 1990s, Thornton and Young-DeMarco (2001) find further evidence of this same trend, particularly regarding high levels of attitudes supporting gender equality within families. They find long-term trends of greater tolerance toward divorce, premarital sex, unmarried cohabitation, remaining single, and choosing not to have children (1009).

Recent changes to work and family life have further contributed to individualization. Individuals must now contend with finding and learning new jobs, as well as shifting family arrangements. Individualization thus requires individuals to manage their careers and family lives more actively. An active approach that requires constant monitoring of social activities and active decision-making about new social actions has been termed "reflexivity." While the use and definition of this term have varied, reflexive awareness of one's social situation at any given moment, and life more broadly, is common to many sociological arguments about the nature of life in service- and knowledge-based economies. In Beck's words,

> Traditional forms of community beyond the family are beginning to disappear. Often, the members of the family choose their own separate relationships and live in networks of their own. This need not imply that social isolation increases or that relatively private family life prevails—although this may happen. But it does imply

that already existing (descriptively organized) neighborhoods are shattered, together with their limitations and their opportunities for social control. The newly formed social relationships and social networks now have to be individually chosen; social ties, too, are becoming reflexive, so that they have to be established, maintained, and constantly renewed by individuals. (Beck 1992, 97)

Central to Beck's theory of individualization is the recognition that individuals are no longer born and socialized into stable social groups. Rather, they actively navigate, maintain, and abandon many kinds of relationships over their lives. While Beck did not frame his argument in this way, his theory ultimately implies that social life now exists in the form of complex, ever-changing and individually centered networks. These networks are complex in that they are decentralized and exist as changing sets of individuals, many of whom are not themselves connected. In the next section, I will discuss three dimensions of personal network complexity.

DIMENSIONS OF PERSONAL NETWORK COMPLEXITY

The individualization described by Beck suggests that the nature of social complexity changed as societies shifted towards complex personal networks. While Coser's notion of social complexity focused on the navigation of clear and widely understood social roles that exist in stable work and family groups—particularly in terms of the rapid shifting between multiple roles throughout the day and the management of role conflicts—Beck's individualization theory implies that roles have become are more ambiguous and individually constructed. This adds another layer of complexity insofar as individuals must not only switch between roles and manage conflict, but they must further reflexively define and articulate social roles to others. Moreover, they must actively maintain relationships in which these roles exist, which gives rise to scheduling complexity. Ultimately, this new type of complexity exists in the form of complex, individually centered personal networks.

Drawing on this sociological literature, I identify three dimensions of personal network complexity: institutional, relational, and temporal. I further consider how power influences these dimensions. As I will show throughout this book, these three dimensions of network complexity, often influenced by power, are configurations that shape practices of connection in the presence of constant connectivity.

Institutional Complexity

Institutional complexity is a critical dimension of personal network complexity. Institutions include all kinds of traditional and nontraditional work and family arrangements. The nature of role complexity within all these arrangements has changed in contemporary personal networks. As work and family arrangements have become more diverse and shorter-lived, role complexity has shifted from having clear expectations that sometimes conflict to dealing with constantly changing and vague expectations. When Coser was developing her theory, role complexity was the result of meeting multiple roles within large and stable organizations. In these roles, individuals were expected to meet different expectations (or "role sets"), depending on who they were interacting with. For example, a manager in a large company was expected to act differently when interacting with other managers, employees directly under their management, employees working under different managers, custodial staff, and members of the board. Coser's assumption was that the organizations were large and centralized enough to employ individuals working in many different roles and that everyone had consistent knowledge about them. Moreover, individuals occupying roles in large organizations typically occupied them for extended periods of time, sometimes for their entire careers.

Individuals now more often move between new and unique family and work arrangements. Given that these institutions are becoming less stable and are taking on a greater variety of configurations, there are more often situations with ambiguous social roles (Hage and Powers

1992). For example, a new designer at a small company may need to carry out tasks relating to management, creation, and customer support. She may be the first person in this type of position at this new company, and so must articulate what her coworkers and clients can expect from her in terms of prioritizing tasks, communication frequency, and response time. Likewise, a divorcée who has recently remarried and has both biological and stepchildren must articulate expectations about daycare with their former and current spouses. This may involve articulating how and when the person and their former spouse should communicate about their children, how often they will communicate, what topics they will discuss and what topics are off limits, how vacations and other irregular events ought to be handled, parenting roles that a new spouse may play, and a number of other issues relating to children and their new relationship as former spouses. Given the lack of widespread and established norms surrounding these arrangements, the need for role articulation is clear.

The rise of single-person households also affects role articulation. Not everyone who lives alone is single, childless, and lacks obligation to their parents and other family members. Rather, not dwelling with family implies a need for actively communicating with family outside the home. Here, too, there seems to be a lack of established relational norms. Individuals who live alone must articulate their role obligations for communication with romantic partners, children, parents, and family members who live separately. They must decide when, how often, and by what medium they communicate. These norms can then be articulated in terms of one's role within a family. For example, should adult children that live alone chat with their parents on a weekly basis? Should these conversations occur via phone calls, video chats, or audio-only chats through messaging apps? Should there first be a text to confirm availability before initiating a call? All these expectations may be made explicit through conversations before routines and expectations are established, or they may evolve more subtly through nonverbal backchanneling or passing comments.

In sum, role articulation is still an important aspect of social life in service and knowledge economies. However, rather than only being a way to resolve role conflicts between clearly defined roles, role articulation is now also a means of dealing with the ambiguity of new and unique family and work arrangements. The constant need for reflexive role articulation is the hallmark of social complexity within individualistic societies. Moreover, closely related to role articulation is the need to actively manage activities and stay in touch with work, family, and friend ties. It is this constant need to actively manage and define expectations for communication and connection that has become a critical dimension of personal network complexity.

Relational Complexity

Somewhat overlapping institutional complexity, but still distinct, relational complexity is another important dimension of personal network complexity. With the increasing complexity within family and work arrangements, the nature of social connection itself has evolved in service- and knowledge-based economies. While it is still true that people maintain a set of strong relationships, weaker relationships have taken a more prominent role in contemporary life. These relationships do not fit neatly into clear and stable social roles of past eras and represent a new dimension of social complexity that was not fully considered in Coser's theoretical framework. In this section, I will review Mark Granovetter's weak ties theory and then consider the implications of his argument for the nature of social complexity.

At more than 63,000 citations, Granovetter's "The Strength of Weak Ties" (1973) is one of the most cited works in social science. The paper makes the elegant and powerful argument that certain types of relationships—namely, strong and weak ties—when coupled with psychological disposition, result in large-scale social structures that influence the flow of information and resources throughout society. Granovetter hypothesized that when someone feels closely connected to two other people that aren't connected, they attempt to achieve psychological balance by connecting them. In contrast, people feel less compelled to connect their weaker relationships to others they know.

Social Configurations

The upshot is that these weak ties tend to be less connected to other people in our personal networks. They swim in different social circles, where they are exposed to different ideas and information. When we connect with these weaker relationships, we are therefore more likely to be exposed to beneficial new ideas and information.

Weak ties are critical for surviving and thriving in service and knowledge economies. Granovetter and others who have drawn on his theory have shown that weak ties can provide valuable information when people are looking for new job opportunities (Granovetter 1995; Erickson 2001). When considering that individuals often change jobs throughout their careers, the importance of weak ties becomes more apparent. In addition to helping individuals find new jobs, weak ties can also help people find new friends and romantic partners. Once again, considering the complexity of family life and the fact that it is more common for individuals to have many romantic partnerships over their lives, it is clear that weak ties are a critical part of life in service- and knowledge-based economies.

While weak ties are now an important part of contemporary life, the strong/weak tie dichotomy glosses over the complexity of tie strength. Granovetter argues that "the strength of a tie is a (probably linear) combination of the amount of time, the emotional intensity, the intimacy (mutual confiding), and the reciprocal services which characterize the tie" (1973, 1361). While this definition has intuitive appeal, "some combination" of these dimensions implies that specific social ties may be strong in some ways and weak in others.

Drawing on personal network questions included in the American General Social Survey, Peter Marsden and Karen E. Campbell (1984) examine how to measure tie strength. Several of their methods tapped into the different dimensions that Granovetter conceptualized. They found two distinct aspects of tie strength: time spent in a relationship and depth of a relationship. They also found that "closeness," or relational intensity, was the best overall indicator of tie strength. These empirical findings confirm that while it may be that relationships are either high or low on all four dimensions that Granovetter conceptualized, many ties do not fit nicely into the strong/weak dichotomy. Depending on the unique, contextual nature of the relationship, relationships might be weak in some ways and strong in others.

Rather than disregard the strong/weak tie dichotomy, a more useful approach would be to acknowledge the complexity of tie strength. Such an approach would accurately represent relationships and accept that people from different social circles play an important role in our lives and in society more broadly. It would allow us to consider that the nature of social relationships is no longer prescribed in clear and stable social roles. Rather, relationships rely on reflexive individuals to infuse them with meaning. This approach is quite consistent with Beck's theory of individualization, in which "life, death, gender, corporeality, identity, religion, marriage, parenthood, *social ties*—are all becoming decidable down to the small print; once fragmented into options, everything must be decided" (Beck and Beck-Gernsheim 2002, 5, italics added). Perhaps what is most important to understand is *why* an individual decides to maintain a relationship and how that relationship helps them thrive within an ever-shifting set of work and family arrangements.

Given that the social complexity discussed by Coser focuses on the management of role conflict, the rising importance of weak ties in which there are no clear role expectations and potentially less role conflict suggests that Coser's theory may be somewhat dated. Nevertheless, the importance of the reflexive awareness in relationships—and the ability to creatively manage relationships in the context of ever-shifting social circumstances—remains consistent with her framework. Individuals articulate certain aspects of their relationships, perhaps not in terms of well-known and agreed-upon social roles but, rather, in the context of their unique relational histories, social circumstances, and desired outcomes. For example, an individual might be interested in reconnecting with an old friend from high school because he was on the job market and felt they could help him discover new job opportunities. He might initiate a conversation in which he was "catching up," express interest in his friend's current career, and then later mention that he was currently on the job market. This type of subtle articulation regarding the explicit and implicit purpose of the interaction requires a high degree of social sensitivity and reflexivity.

Social Configurations

In short, the complexity of social ties defines life in service- and knowledge-based economies because it is how reflexive agency provides individuals with the means of navigating changing institutional arrangements. The increasing importance of complex and multidimensional weak ties further suggests that navigating social complexity now requires even greater levels of reflexive awareness, social skill, and active maintenance of weak tie relationships.

Temporal Complexity

A third dimension of personal network complexity is temporal complexity. In terms of work life, downsizing and the increasing prevalence of small and medium service businesses has coincided with the rise of "just-in-time" approaches to coordinating work-related activities. The process of producing services requires organizations to coordinate with other organizations. For knowledge workers in mid- and upper-level positions within these organizations, this has meant an increase in the complexity of scheduling logistics and constant communication with copresent and distant others.

In a study of knowledge workers at a large multinational communication company, Judy Wajcman (2015) finds that workers spent nearly half of their work time communicating with others. About half of that time spent communicating was mediated via email and telephone calls. Overall interactions (mediated and in-person) were short, lasting between five and seven minutes. Interestingly, Wajcman finds that, while much of a worker's day is spent communicating, these communication events were often initiated by workers themselves, rather than being forced on them. To Wajcman, this self-direction indicates that workers "are actively negotiating a whole new communication repertoire and deploying them as everyday tools."

The temporal complexity of Wajcman's workplace points to the reflexive nature of contemporary knowledge and service organizations, in which workers must constantly decide with whom to communicate, what tasks to perform, and when to carry out their tasks. This type of complexity is akin to the type of social complexity discussed by Coser, in that individuals must actively switch between various roles while at work. However, the focus on actively choosing to initiate most activities may be more intense and reflexive than activities carried out in more structured and large organizations that Coser discussed. In this way, complexity arises not only from the lack of structured routines but also from constantly prioritizing activities and adjusting quickly to changes and new demands. Lack of job certainty and long-term work arrangements exacerbate this condition. Workers not only need to keep up with the demands of their jobs but must constantly be on the lookout for new job opportunities and avenues for career development.

The complexity of organizations and their workflows has also impacted low-wage, low-skilled workers. While low-wage goods-producing workers have regular shifts at factories or in other large organizations, low-wage service workers are increasingly more likely to receive assignments directly from digital platforms. Delivery people, "ride share" service drivers, temporary laborers, and other "gig economy" workers can only choose to accept or reject jobs; they have little choice over timing. Even when workers choose to reject a job, they understand that their choice may lead to fewer or less desirable jobs. Once a job has been accepted, instructions (such as where to drive and what route to take) are often provided by the platform. There is little room for even the smallest amount of choice in how or exactly when work is performed. In short, platform labor has become "simpler" insofar as individuals have fewer choices in how and when work is performed. Nevertheless, the temporal rhythms of low-status work are now more difficult to predict and control (Chen and Sun 2020).

The lack of autonomy over one's time faced by gig workers does not differ greatly from the demands that low-skilled service workers have traditionally faced. For example, Sarah Sharma's (2014) ethnographic study of taxi drivers conducted before the development of ride-sharing platforms showed how drivers lacked autonomy over where and when they work. The complexity they faced wasn't the result of them reflexively choosing between possible tasks or people with whom to communicate. Drawing a contrast between the working conditions faced by "jet-lagged" professionals, Sharma argues that taxi drivers are "cab-lagged"; they must keep up with the time demands of others. As Sharma puts it, "Cab lag, then, refers to a condition of labor of where people exist in a differential and inequitable temporal relation with another group with whom they are expected to sync up . . . . Cab-lagged populations do have a relationship to the dominant temporal infrastructure. They clean, service, and maintain it" (80). She implies that while knowledge workers and other professionals of the jet-lagged class deal with complexity reflexively, workers in low-status positions also deal with complexity in terms of accommodating the unpredictable and often rushed requirements of others.

As a result of increasing complexity in workflow logistics, workers are now less likely to adhere to a standard forty-hour work week. The blurring of home and work life is now more common, and workers are likely to work at odd hours, often in their own homes. More flexible or nonstandard work hours further add to the complexity of arranging household activities between spouses and partners and activities between families spread throughout multiple households. The growing prevalence of nonnuclear family arrangements—such as shared custody situations in which children move between two homes—further requires the coordination of visits and travel arrangements.

At the time of Coser's writing, the coordination of activities at work and home required individuals to share rigid schedules. Inflexibility had the effect of separating social roles: "Through the territorial and temporal separation of activities . . . the individual is insulated not only from observability by role partners in the other set, but also from their authority and their interest. A woman cannot tell her husband how to behave on the job, nor can his employer tell him how to behave at home" (Coser 1991, 116). With the blurring of work and family life, and the loosening of work schedules, individuals now actively manage expectations at work and home. They must decide how and when they interact with family and colleagues in both locations. This adds a new dimension to personal network complexity, in that individuals must be reflexively aware of their current circumstances at work and home and manage communication expectations in both settings.

POWER AND PERSONAL NETWORK COMPLEXITY

Having explored three dimensions of personal network complexity, I will now discuss how power and inequality influence the extent to which individuals can manage these types of complexity. I draw again Coser's theory, as it provides a way of understanding the relationship between role complexity, power, and systematic inequality.

As discussed earlier, Coser argues that role complexity is the hallmark of modern life. She further argues that occupying several roles allows individuals to exercise personal autonomy, especially when these roles involve contradictory expectations. According to Coser, the level of power provided by social roles determines whether an individual can exercise autonomy in resolving role conflict. If their roles do not provide them with the power to resolve these conflicts, they must endure the stress and possible sanctions involved in not meeting the expectations of their roles. For example, conflict might occur when a salesperson is asked by their manager to meet a new potential client at a time when they had instead planned to catch up on a backlog of existing work. The salesperson has power in this situation if they have the autonomy to turn down their manager's request and determine their own schedule.

In addition to the power of roles, I would add that support, information, and resources also help individuals act autonomously when role conflict arises. While support, information, and resources can exist independently of social roles, they are often directly tied to roles within the family and at work. High-status occupations generally bring high levels of income and benefits such as sick leave, along with social roles that provide the ability to control one's own schedule. Individuals in these occupations often have skills, education, and social connections that help them to find useful information. Within families, certain roles are more likely to bring financial or emotional support, while others are more likely to require giving support.

The separation of work and family and the development of complex organizations brought an uneven distribution of social equality. Coser's theory of power and autonomy is deeply connected to systematic gender and class inequalities. Regarding gender, roles that women occupy

Social Configurations

in family and work institutions that provide them with only simple role sets do not give them the means to articulate their roles and exercise their autonomy. Within family institutions, feminized roles (e.g., mother, daughter, and wife roles) often provide less decision-making power than masculine roles. Moreover, as women have faced unequal barriers in entering and succeeding in the workforce, they often have fewer roles and simpler role sets than men. When conflicts between work and family arise, differing cultural expectations surrounding these roles mean that women often have unequal power to manage them. As Coser explains,

> In all likelihood it will be the mother, not the father, who will stay home for the sick child, and it will be the father, not the mother, who will give to the job the weekend time usually assigned to the family. The choice between two activity systems follows a preferential cultural pattern. The woman has the cultural mandate to give priority to the family. Even when working outside the home, she is expected to be committed to her family first, her work second, and this helps prevent disruptions within the family. (118)

Toward the end of her book, Coser recognized the changing status of women when she was writing in the early 1990s. While there have been significant changes in the roles that women have occupied within family and work institutions, it is clear that gender inequality remains, and Coser's writings on this subject are unfortunately still relevant.

Regarding social class, Coser focuses on the relationship between role complexity and alienation. She argues that low status typically restricts the range of a person's behaviors and interaction partners. These restricted role sets provide individuals with little room to act creatively and exercise power during role conflicts. This lack of autonomy is one source of alienation whereby people feel estranged and powerless at work. Restricted role sets also mean that those working in low-status jobs interact mostly with each other or managers. This gives workers little opportunity to challenge or articulate their roles, as the constant interaction with those in the same role and managers only reinforces explicit expectations about routine behaviors.

Coser expands this argument beyond "blue collar" factory work to involve a wide range of low-status roles that exist in complex organizations. Her argument is based mainly on an empirical study of nurses, doctors, and staff working at a large hospital. She finds that nurses tend to experience a strong sense of anomie due to the routinized nature of working with restricted role sets. While they don't often report experiencing situations of acute stress, their stress comes from more of a general sense of routine and highly defined expectations that limit their articulation of themselves in relation to their work.

Although roles have become more ambiguous in the context of institutional and relational complexity, the extent to which individuals have the power to articulate, redefine, or ignore social expectations remains linked to their status within work and family institutions. In fact, the power and autonomy to manage expectations defines social life in service- and knowledge-based economies. As a result of these changing attitudes, social roles within families are less taken for granted than they once were. The relatively new possibility of divorce has provided both a means of exiting traditional arrangements and decreasing dependency on problematic marriages. This has meant that couples must more actively negotiate their roles regarding household duties and child care. Nevertheless, while attitudes may have generally changed, gender inequalities within families persist (Kane and Sanchez 1994). This persistence may be particularly true in families where women have relatively lower levels of education and limited career options, making them more financially dependent on their spouses. The point being made here is that compared to early and preindustrialization, the very possibility of divorce is likely to have resulted in an increased need for role articulation.

Gender and economic inequalities manifest through role articulation and family conflict. Within marriages, a spouse may be less likely to engage in role articulation or challenge unwanted demands from their partners if a resulting divorce could leave them destitute. Given gender inequalities in the workforce (Kalev and Deutsch 2018), power

Social Configurations

inequalities within marriages tend to burden women more than men. Moreover, there has been a recent abrupt increase in the portion of young adult children living with their parents (Vanorman and Jacobsen 2020) due to the increasing cost of living in service economies. Such financial inequalities are the result of unequal power between generations, which may manifest inequality as adult children and parents attempt to articulate their roles in these newly emerging situations. Considering that a high cost of living burdens low-income workers the most, these types of role conflicts are most likely to manifest in low-income families. Finally, tensions can arise with parents as teens attempt to establish more independent roles within the family. Attempts to establish greater independence are the first times that individuals attempt to articulate their roles, and this articulation can lead to conflict when they don't align with parents' expectations. Here, too, low-income families may acutely experience these conflicts, given that both parents and children in these families may be less accustomed to articulating expectations in ways that minimize conflict.

At the time of Coser's writing, many countries were in the process of shifting to a service-based economy. Factories were still commonplace, as were the large and complex hierarchical organizations that ran them. Coser's discussion of social class was based on typifying jobs as being either blue collar factory positions or white-collar management positions. With the offshoring of factory production, this typology became less useful to describe jobs in knowledge and service economies. However, Coser's argument was not necessarily about the exact duties performed or the output of the work organizations. Rather, Coser focused on how the complexity of social roles varied between jobs of different statuses and incomes. Her concern with the extent to which different types of jobs required individuals to switch between role sets and articulate their roles in the face of role conflict remains highly useful, particularly when considering the rise of platform-based service labor.

While factory jobs declined in service-based economies, low-wage jobs still typically require only simple role sets. An extreme example of this is the rise of ride sharing, delivery, and other platformed-based "just-in-time" jobs. In these jobs, workers often receive instructions directly from platforms through mobile app–based technology. Conflict can arise when a platform assigns tasks that are unreasonable—such as delivering a package at a particular time when unexpected traffic is too heavy—or conflict with existing commitments (Chen and Sun 2020). There is also minimal or sometimes no interaction with clients and others working for the same platform. Such conflicts leave workers with little opportunity to articulate their roles as a means of resolving conflicts.

PERSONAL NETWORK COMPLEXITY AND THE CONFIGURATION APPROACH

Before concluding, it is important to make clear exactly how the personal network complexity is central to contemporary social configurations. Drawing on Giddens's (1984) structuration theory, I argued in the previous chapter that social configurations are rules and resources that allow individuals to carry out social actions. I have argued that social roles tend to be more individually determined as economies become knowledge and service oriented. However, this is not to say that roles now lack any rules, but rather, that individuals tend to have more influence in determining these rules in the context of institutions, relationships, and the temporal flow of social interactions. This is particularly true when they occupy roles that provide them with the power to make these determinations. Network complexity is central to contemporary social configurations because it requires that individuals actively construct and manage their social roles.

We can expect that individuals living in countries with economies that are primarily knowledge and service oriented will tend to have more personal network complexity than those living in countries that are primarily industrial. However, even in countries that are primarily industrial, individuals working outside of industry may still have complex personal networks. Moreover, within countries with primarily knowledge and service economies, those working in traditional industries (such as manufacturing or agriculture) and those working in large

Social Configurations

and stable public sector occupations may have networks that lack high amounts of institutional, relational, and temporal complexity.

CONCLUSION

At the outset of this chapter, I asked, What are the commonly occurring social and technological configurations that enable and constrain practices of connection? Addressing the first part of this question, I have argued that these commonly occurring social configurations take the form of personal network complexity. Personal networks are complexly configured in that individuals often need to reflexively choose and develop social rules as a means of navigating shifting work and family institutions, relationships, and the temporal flow of interactions.

What does social complexity mean for the social implications of constant connectivity? As I argued in the previous chapter, the social implications of constant connectivity take the form of mediated practices of connection that occur within social and technological configurations. Knowing that contemporary social configurations tend be complex helps us to understand the context in which practices of connection are developed. Following the logic of the configuration approach, we can then expect that commonly occurring practices of connection will help to maintain and perpetuate complexly configured personal networks.

In the next chapter, I will address the second part of the question posed regarding commonly occurring technological configurations that enable and constrain practices of connection.

4

Technological Configurations

In the previous chapter, I asked, What are the commonly occurring social and technological configurations that enable and constrain practices of connection? I then addressed the first part of this question by drawing on social theory to discuss several dimensions of personal network complexity. In this chapter, I will address the second part of this question by discussing three dimensions of mediated communication complexity. As with social configurations, these technological configurations have become increasingly complex over time. Considering the complex nature of contemporary mediated communication technology will help us to understand the technological context in which individuals develop practices of connection in the presence of constant connectivity.

THE DEVELOPMENT OF COMPLEX COMMUNICATION TECHNOLOGY

While not commonly thought as a communication technology, the emergence of mass transportation infrastructures during industrialization influenced possibilities for in-person communication. By allowing for more rapid movement between rural and newly developing urban areas, transportation technologies such as the railways and roadways extended the range of individuals with whom in-person interactions were possible. Rather than people being bounded by smaller rural communities, these transportation technologies enabled the growth of urban

The Digital Bind. Jeffrey Boase, Oxford University Press. © Oxford University Press (2025).
DOI: 10.1093/oso/9780197798591.003.0005

areas built around the emerging industrial complex. As discussed in the previous chapter, early industrialized urban life decoupled work and family institutions, allowing for more complex social roles that individuals moved between in their everyday lives.

The development of more complex and extensive transportation networks during industrialization also facilitated the development of postal systems. In turn, the development of postal systems subsidized and justified the development of transportation systems. In the nineteenth and early twentieth centuries, industrializing countries such as Great Britain and the United States invested heavily in the development of postal services, an investment that enabled public access. For example, the US postal service was heavily developed in the second half of the eighteenth century under the direction of its head postmaster general, Benjamin Franklin. By 1901, 76,945 post offices had been established, which attracted more widespread and heavy usage. For example, the annual revenue for the postal system increased nearly 45 times between 1790 and 1839 (Brix 2022).

The heavy adoption of postal services by the general public enabled the exchange of physical artifacts (often letters) between fixed locations, which enabled the coordination of activities and maintenance of relationships with distant others. It also allowed for the exchange of resources through money orders and the exchange of other valuable items. While the speed of delivery and cost limited how the exchange of artifacts could be used to maintain geographically distant relationships, mass diffusion of postal services enabled the possibility of maintaining relationships that otherwise may have withered or become lost due to a lack of communication. In certain cases, it may have also facilitated relational development, such as when someone with whom there was a newly established relationship moved to another city.

The infrastructural development of the telegraph in the mid- to late nineteenth century increased the speed of long-distance communication between fixed locations. Initially used for sending and receiving Morse code, this system was extensively employed by military organizations rather than the general public. However, by the early twentieth century, the development of the telegraph—a device that allowed typewritten messages to be exchanged at 500 characters a minute—facilitated more widespread use of the technology among the general public. Unlike postal delivery, which enabled the slow transfer of artifacts between fixed locations, the telegraph allowed for the reproduction of text-based artifacts, thereby increasing the speed of communication. Nevertheless, the cost and size of these machines prevented them from becoming household items. They were often located in post offices and larger organizations such as news agencies (Bruno 2004).

The diffusion of the telephone began at the same time as the telegraph, in the first half of the twentieth century, and many large telephone companies began as telegraph operations. Although the telephone was originally marketed as a business tool, Claude Fischer's (1992) social history of the telephone shows that it was quickly recognized by the public as being a device for socialization. Drawing on interviews and historic materials, Fischer finds that the telephone both allowed people to maintain relationships with those who lived in other neighborhoods and towns and reinforced local relationships. In his words, "Focusing on personal matters, the home telephone seems to have added considerable convenience and security. It also seems to have expanded the dimensions of social life, the realm of frequent checking-in, rapid updates, easy scheduling of appointments, and quick exchanges of casual confidences, as well as the sphere of long-distance conversation. No doubt, such social calls have displaced some face-to-face contacts (as well as letter-writing), but overall, total talk has most surely expanded" (p. 268).

Returning to the design elements of communication technology, the landline telephone was one of the first widely available technologies that enabled ephemeral voice-based interaction between fixed locations. It diffused at a time when people spent most of their waking hours in two locations: home and work. Public telephone booths also provided the opportunity to engage in this type of communication, although they were still constrained to areas with high levels of foot traffic. Despite locational constraints, the opportunity to engage in voice-based exchanges allowed for the rapid exchange of rich information between individuals. When considering that telephones diffused widely in countries

Technological Configurations

in which there were enduring work and family institutions—in which individuals lived and worked in the same locations for long periods of times—it becomes clear that there was congruence between the locational constraints of telephones and the social roles of those using them.

Given that landline telephones were often located in homes and workplaces, their use often did not offer a high degree of individual privacy. Although phone calls were typically between just two individuals, auditory and locational constraints meant that others living or working in the same place would know that a call was taking place and might overhear part of the conversation. Even when individuals make calls in their own bedrooms or private offices, those working or living with them may at least be aware that they are unavailable because they are on the phone. In this way, the constraints of landline phones aligned them with stable home and work institutions, while the possibility of finding times for private or semiprivate conversations provided opportunities for developing relationships outside of these institutions.

Other communication technologies such as fax machines and pagers diffused in the second half of the twentieth century, although they were not as widely adopted as telephones. Fax machines were mostly adopted within office settings, while pagers were typically used by high-status professionals. Given this book's focus on technologies used by the general public, it may suffice to say that these technologies expanded the range of communication options available for some. However, the range of communication options expanded even more with the diffusion of the personal computer, mobile phones, and the internet.

PERSONAL COMPUTERS AND THE INTERNET

While personal computers became widely adopted in the 1980s and 1990s, the general public did not generally use them for direct person-to-person communication until the diffusion of the internet in the late 1990s and early 2000s.[1] Email was the first medium to use this system and be adopted by the general public. At first only used by militaries, governments, and other larger organizations, the development of browser-based webmail systems and email clients in the mid-1990s allowed email to gain traction among the public by the late 1990s (PR Newswire 2021). While email is now considered somewhat prosaic, it's important to recognize that it became one of the most rapidly diffusing communication technologies in history. As of 2001, we sent 296.3 billion emails per day, and almost 1 in 5 people use Gmail (PR Newswire 2021).

Email employed several unique design elements that set it apart from other technologies at the time. As a visually based medium, it allowed for written exchanges that were sent directly between individual accounts. Temporally, it was designed such that copies of messages written by a sender would be reproduced for one or many receivers. Unlike regular postal mail, messages are received as soon as they are sent, enabling either rapid or slow exchanges. It's also notable that these exchanges came at no cost, even when they were sent between individuals living in different parts of the world—although the costs of purchasing a personal computer and paying for a monthly internet connection were significant.

Email is among the first widely adopted communication technologies with design elements that provide several opportunities for communication that is useful when maintaining complex personal networks. The direct and visual nature of the medium allows for individualized social exchanges that can occur unbeknownst to others in the same home or workplace. The instant reproduction of digital artifacts in the form of messages and attachments also means that individuals can exchange messages without interrupting those around them. This design element is particularly useful to individuals who must manage communications with multiple weaker relationships with whom there may be no known or mutually convenient time for ephemeral exchanges (i.e., phone calls). Further, the ability to exchange messages without regard to distance further makes email useful for those who wish to maintain connections with people who live elsewhere.

While email was diffusing in the 1990s and early 2000s, other internet-based media were beginning to gain users. While SMS texting is currently considered to be limited to mobile devices, instant messaging was common on computers during this time. In 2004 I codeveloped a survey of American adults that was funded by the Pew Internet & American Life project (Boase et al. 2006). In this survey, we found that 39% of our respondents had used computer-based instant messaging in the past month. Of those respondents, 65% used instant messaging to connect with a very close relationship at least weekly, and 35% used it to connect with a somewhat close relationship at least weekly. Overall, these results showed us that a significant number of American adults were using instant messaging, usually to connect with their strongest relationships.

As with email, the design elements of instant messaging were congruent with the type of relational maintenance and development required by individuals navigating more fluid family and work institutions. Also similar to email, instant messaging allowed for the exchange of digital artifacts in the form of text messages directly between individuals. This allowed for communication between individuals in work or home settings where telephones might be considered disruptive. Moreover, while the computers used to exchange messages weren't portable, messages could be exchanged instantly and without cost, regardless of geographic distance. Such design elements allowed for the maintenance of relationships over time, even as individuals moved to different neighborhoods, cities, or countries.

In the early 2000s, web-based social media sites also made their first appearance.[2] Social media sites such as Friendster launched in 2002, followed MySpace in 2003, Facebook and Orkut in 2004, and Twitter in 2006 (Edwards 2011). At launch, access to these sites was exclusively through personal computers, and mobile access did not occur until the diffusion of the iPhone in 2007. While there were many design differences between these sites, they all shared certain core elements. danah boyd and Nicole Ellison (2007) identified these design elements as (1) public or semipublic user profiles, (2) a list of other profiles with which users could connect, and (3) the ability to view the connections made by others. The use of these sites was visual in nature and enabled the sharing of digital artifacts such as photos and message posts between specific individuals or friend groups.

Social media sites shared many design features with email and instant messaging that allowed users to instantly exchange visual artifacts.[3] However, the profile feature allowed individuals to locate others by searching for their names or traversing common profile connections. This feature was particularly useful for individuals wishing to connect with new or weaker relationships, as adding a friend did not require the exchange of email addresses or telephone numbers. Additionally, while both email and social media sites allowed individuals to share a single digital artifact with many other people, email required specific individuals to be identified as recipients. Social media sites allowed users to post artifacts without specifying who would view them. This design feature made these sites useful for those who wished to nurture new relationships, in which direct emailing may have been considered inappropriate or too forward.

In sum, the mass diffusion of personal computers and internet access allowed for the adoption of several new communication media. Although initially limited to fixed desktop computers, new forms of communication allowed for more individualized communication. These communication technologies were particularly useful for developing and maintaining relationships both inside and outside of core family and work institutions. They enabled instant exchange of visual digital artifacts within systems that could only be accessed directly by individual accounts, potentially unbeknownst to those in the same households and workplaces. These artifacts could be exchanged regardless of distance and viewed at times that did not necessarily interrupt the flow of activities in the way that an ephemeral phone call might.

Despite congruency between these internet-based media and individualistic social complexity, the fact that they were primarily accessed through stationary computers and using web browsers created certain constraints. As individuals moved between different locations throughout their day, they were unable to access these media. While they could potentially hide some of their communications by accessing individual accounts, their computer monitors could potentially be seen by others, meaning their communications would not be fully private. Finally, at the time, many people did not have access to personal computers in their workplaces. The cost of purchasing a personal computer and home internet connectivity meant that most people had only limited access to internet-based communication media. It was not until the diffusion of smartphones that these communication constraints began to loosen.

THE MOBILE TURN

At the same time that personal computers and fixed internet connections became broadly adopted in the 1990s, mobile phones were diffusing rapidly. By most measures, mobile phones were diffusing more rapidly around the globe than personal computers or other current or previous technology (Comer and Wikle 2008). However, at this time most phones only allowed for voice calling, and it was not until the late 1990s and early 2000s they allowed for SMS texting (Agar 2003). These messages could only be exchanged between mobile phones and typically required entry through numeric keypads. This process was relatively slow compared to more typical keyboard or current touchscreen entry, and exchange of messages using this system was mostly done by younger adults in countries like Japan and Scandinavian countries (Agar 2003). By the mid-2000s, a relatively small number of individuals were adopting mobiles with tactile keyboards and internet service. However, the cost of these devices and internet mobile phone plans meant that most of these early adopters were young professionals. In short, while mobile phones became widely adopted in the 1990s and early 2000s, their functionality was mostly limited to voice calling for a majority of those who owned them. The portability of these devices was critical to the development of the constant connectivity, and it increased individualization and private communication compared to landline phones that were typically located in homes and workplaces.

It was not until the rapid diffusion of smartphones and the mass expansion of mobile internet services in the late 2000s and 2010s that mobile devices became a primary way to access increasingly complex communication media. Smartphones represented an important technological development because they offered the possibility of installing software applications (or "apps"), which used mobile internet connectivity to enable a variety of mediated interactions. Moreover, development of touchscreen, camera, and microphone technologies aided in the production of digital artifacts—pictures, videos, text, and emojis—while still allowing for ephemeral audio and video exchanges.

At the time of this writing, these media can be roughly divided into stand-alone texting and messaging apps, social media feed apps, and multimedia (audio and video) apps. However, the large amount of variation in these apps, and their ever-changing nature, means it is impossible to concisely describe their communication features in an enduring way. Instead, in this chapter, I will discuss the complex qualities of communication technologies at the time of this writing in the early 2020s. Although much of this discussion will focus on smartphone-based communication, as I will argue, the distinction between communication occurring on these devices, personal computers, and wearable devices has become blurred—also a by-product of technological complexity. The purpose of discussing these dimensions of communication technology complexity is to outline how this complexity manifests and to provide a set of dimensions that are unlikely to change in the near future, even as the specific technologies themselves change.

THE POSTSMARTPHONE ERA

Smartphones are likely to remain widely used for several more years, if not decades. Yet new technologies that will significantly alter and perhaps replace the use of these smartphones are already on the horizon. Wearable devices—particularly watches—that connect directly to the internet are becoming increasingly common. Technology companies are

Technological Configurations

investing heavily in eyewear that connects directly to the internet and allows individuals to augment and modify their visual fields with graphical and textual information. While it is possible that individuals may continue to carry devices for entering or searching information in situations that do not allow doing so through the use of voice recognition, smartphone devices that require individuals to gaze downward may eventually be unnecessary and undesired. Eventually wearable technology may bypass sense organs and interface directly with the nervous system and brain (Vaughan et al. 2003). All of these technologies are currently being researched, and the components for their existence are being developed.

Whatever formats mobile technology takes moving forward, the potential for constant connectivity will remain. There is little reason to believe that the potential for individuals to be connected to the digital world through devices on or attached to their persons will disappear. It may be the case that certain groups will avoid using this technology—much as the Amish population avoids using cars today. It is also highly likely that massive disparities between populations will mean that these technologies will not be equally spread through the world's population at any given time. If the constant connectivity disappeared, it would likely be due to a complete reorganization of global societies, the format of which would be impossible to predict with any confidence at this point in history.

DIMENSIONS OF MEDIATED COMMUNICATION COMPLEXITY

My argument in this book is mainly concerned with technological complexity as it exists in present-day communication technologies. In this section, I will discuss three dimensions of this type of technological complexity: the variety of communication apps and devices, the variety of communicative options within apps, and the changing nature of apps and devices.

Variety of Communication Apps and Devices

One critical dimension of technological complexity that provides opportunities and constraints for communication is the wide variety of communication apps and devices available to individuals. The development of app-centered mobile devices, broadband wireless internet infrastructure, and platform-based services have enabled an extensive array of communication options. Individuals can now install a multitude of platform-based apps, each of which has its own communication functionality.[4] There are several ways of thinking about and categorizing these types of communicative functionality. For example, in a discussion of app media, Gerard Goggin has identified these communicative functions as including quotidian voice media and message media (2021). Another way to think of this functionality is by distinguishing between ephemeral and artifact-based media. Bernie Hogan (2010) applied this distinction in the context of social media platforms, and it can be applied here to understand two broad types of communicative functionality. Ephemeral media—such as voice and video calls—require that two or more individuals communicate synchronously. In contrast, media designed for the exchange of digital artifacts take the form of symbols (text and emojis), pictures, videos, and audio messages.

Many of these apps offer the same basic functionality in terms of allowing for ephemeral and artifact-based exchanges, but often with somewhat different configurations. For example, people can install several different types of messaging apps on the same mobile device. Many of these apps will have the same basic functionality—the exchange of messages. However, there will still be some functional differences between them. Some messaging apps provide the option of having messages disappear after they have been viewed, while others do not. Others messaging apps may be closely integrated to social media feeds, such that users can easily link social media posts to messages. In short, the proliferation of communication apps that have some but not all overlapping functionality has created an extensive constellation of communication possibilities. Within this constellation, individuals can access many

Technological Configurations

types of uniquely configured apps and connect with different sets of individuals or groups.

In addition to the variety of communication apps available, the sheer variety of devices in which these apps can be installed is a closely related source of technological complexity. Individuals are now able to access the same platform using many different types of devices because they are connected directly to systems through always-on mobile internet services. For example, it is possible to access the same message through mobile devices, personal computers, and apps installed on wearable devices. Several devices owned by the same individual can coordinate sequences of communication, such as when a watch notifies the wearer of a new message through a haptic tapping, and the user then reads and responds to this message on their mobile phone.

On the one hand, the ability to use several different devices to communicate within a specific platform can help to simplify the communication process insofar as access to contact information and communication histories is available across multiple devices. On the other hand, access to the same platform through multiple devices can create situational complexity. For example, before the connection of multiple devices through a single platform, when video calls occurred between two desktop computers, the person initiating the call could expect that the individual receiving it would be at a particular location. This would influence their expectations for how this interaction would progress. In contrast, if the person receives a video call on their phone while they are driving, this will very much modify and (hopefully) constrain the interaction. Not knowing the device on which a communication will be received means the context of interaction is also unknown, adding to the complexity of mediated exchanges.

Table 4.1 shows the multitude of communication apps used by the 110 respondents who were interviewed in the study that will be discussed in Part II of this book. This list is by no means exhaustive, nor does it list the many communication features some of these apps include, such as feeds, stories, reposting, forwarding, and if messages have been seen or read. Moreover, given that these apps often add new functionality, the

Table 4.1. APPS USED BY STUDY PARTICIPANTS AND THEIR FUNCTIONALITY FOR DIRECT COMMUNICATION BETWEEN INDIVIDUALS

	Artifact				Ephemeral	
	Text messages	Pictures	Voice messages	Video messages	Voice	Video
Mobile calling			✓		✓	
Default mobile texting	✓	✓	✓	✓		
FaceTime					✓	✓
Skype	✓			✓	✓	✓
Email	✓	✓	✓	✓		
Facebook Messenger	✓	✓	✓		✓	✓
WhatsApp	✓	✓	✓	✓	✓	✓
Instagram	✓	✓	✓	✓	✓	✓
SnapChat	✓	✓	✓	✓	✓	✓
Sales Force	✓	✓	✓	✓	✓	✓
Slack	✓	✓	✓	✓	✓	✓
Zoom	✓	✓		✓	✓	✓
Twitter	✓	✓		✓	✓	✓
Discord	✓	✓		✓	✓	✓
MS Teams	✓	✓	✓	✓	✓	✓
Workplace	✓	✓	✓	✓		
WeChat	✓	✓	✓	✓	✓	✓
Webex	✓	✓		✓	✓	✓
LinkedIn	✓	✓				
Chili Piper	✓	✓			✓	✓
Line	✓	✓	✓	✓	✓	✓
Reddit	✓	✓		✓		
Tumblr	✓	✓	✓	✓		
Pinterest	✓	✓	✓			
Google Meet		✓			✓	✓
Signal	✓	✓	✓	✓	✓	✓
Viber	✓	✓	✓	✓	✓	✓

functionality included in this table is current only as of 2022. However, even noting only basic functionality, this table provides a sense of the extensive number of communication options available during this time period.

Variety of Communication Options within Apps

Another important dimension of technological complexity that provides opportunities and constraints for communication is the extensive array of communication options available within particular apps. Within a single app, it is often possible to carry out ephemeral interactions through voice calls and video calls and exchange artifact-based voice, video, photo, and text messages. These ephemeral and artifact-based interactions can happen one on one or as groups—for example, through group calls or group message threads. In this way, a complex array of options may be available in a single app.

While several apps offer similar arrays of communication options, apps often differentiate themselves by providing unique combinations of these options. For example, some apps might offer artifact-based text messaging but not ephemeral video or voice calling. Other apps might offer ephemeral video calling but not artifact-based voice and video messages. The complexity of communication options within apps arises not only from the fact that a single app may permit a wide variety of communicative functions but also from the fact that the combination of communication options in an app sets it apart from other apps.

The Changing Nature of Apps and Devices

A final dimension of technological complexity that constrains and enables communication is the changing nature of apps and devices. Unlike hardware-based media such as landline phones, software-based communication apps can be installed, uninstalled, upgraded, and phased out. Such flexibility has meant that platform-based apps can offer and remove communication functionality over time. The frequent changing of functionality and interface options is a key element of social media platforms with which users must contend (Bucher and Helmond 2017).

Communication functionality can also be removed from platform-based apps, and in some cases platforms can disappear altogether. For example, Facebook offered users the option of "poking" someone on their contact list. When this function was used, the individual who was "poked" would receive a notification indicating which individual had carried out this action. After an unsuccessful revival in 2017, this feature was buried within a website sidebar and was eventually removed from the interface, effectively making it invisible to users (Notopoulos 2022). Software-based communication apps can also become obsolete or be abandoned altogether, as was the case with the social networking service Orkut, owned and operated by Google. Orkut was one of the most visited websites in India and Brazil in 2008; however, Google closed Orkut completely in 2014.

Communication hardware has also been evolving rapidly, as mobile devices continue to house more powerful components such as faster internet modems, high-resolution cameras, and larger and brighter screens. These changes have increased the range of communication activities that are possible on these devices. At the time of this writing, it has recently become common for people to use their mobiles for video calls and to synchronously exercise with friends and family members worldwide.

As processing and sensor components have become more powerful, they have also become smaller. Shrinking form factors have enabled the development of new portable devices that can be used for communication. Currently, watches can notify users of new phone calls, messages, and social media posts through haptic taps. These watches currently have the ability to connect directly to the internet through cellular signals and enable users to act on these notifications, as well as phone calls, without being tethered to a nearby mobile phone. Tech companies

Technological Configurations   89

are continuing to develop other wearable technologies that can perform tasks such as augmenting vision by visually notifying users of new communication events. It is quite likely that at some point in the coming decades these devices will overlay visual information during in-person interactions, such that an interlocutor's name or other personal information may appear within the wearer's vision during interactions. The constellation of communication options available to individuals is continually evolving, adding to the complexity of an already nebulous array of communication options.

MEDIATED COMMUNICATION COMPLEXITY AND THE CONFIGURATION APPROACH

Before closing, we should consider how it is that the dimensions of mediated communication complexity that I have outlined in this chapter can be thought of as technological configurations. In the second chapter, I defined technological configurations as rules and resources embedded into hardware and software that influence how technology acts. In the case of communication apps and devices, these rules consist of software protocols, algorithms, and hardware design.

In this chapter, I have discussed how the hardware and software involved in the development of mediated communication technologies have become increasingly complex since industrialization, evolving from transportation and postal systems to the complex array of communication options that are currently available. The inner workings of present-day communication technologies have also become more complex in that they consist of many recursive layers and combinations of subcomponents (Arthur 2009). The subcomponents consist of many algorithms and protocols running on many hardware components within both personal devices and the telecommunication networks that connect these devices.

All three dimensions of mediated communication complexity discussed in this chapter involve communication apps. As best described by Goggin (2021), "apps are software that rests upon layers of other software, all ultimately written in code, and all collectively drive the machine of smartphone and other devices to undertake what Lucy Suchman famously called 'situated actions' (Suchman, 2006)." In other words, running even a single communication app involves a high degree of technological complexity, as it requires many layers of scripts and algorithms. Consider too that many communications apps work by connecting via the internet to platforms. These platforms are composed of complex algorithms that run on servers as a means of controlling and orchestrating the actions of device-based apps. All of this shows how app-based mediated communication is complexly configured. When further considering the wide variety of communication apps being used today, each with its unique set of communicative functions, and that new apps are constantly being developed, the complexity of these software configurations is even more apparent.

Complexity also exists within the physical devices that run apps. These devices involve complex assortments of components, including chips, RAM, screens, storage, and so on. These complex hardware configurations that were once limited to stationary desktop computers now exist within most portable devices, such as smartphones and wearables. Given that each of these devices is complexly configured, and that there is a wide variety of devices currently used and being developed, it is clear that the hardware side of mediated communication depends heavily on complex technological configurations.

CONCLUSION

At the start of this chapter, I opened with the question, What are the social and technological configurations that enable and constrain mediated communication practices in the presence of constant connectivity? In the previous chapter, I argued that the social configurations that enable and constrain these practices take the form of complex social configurations. In this chapter, I addressed the second part of this question by arguing that the technological configurations that enable and constrain these practices take the form of complexly configured mediated communication technologies. In short, both social and technological configurations are complex in their own particular ways.

The configuration approach leads us to expect a congruence between technical and social configurations. This is because the practices that occur within these configurations will typically be successful if they allow social and technological order to be reproduced. What this means in the case of personal network complexity is that people will find ways to draw on mediated communication that allow them to maintain institutional, relational, and temporal complexity. In the case of mediated communication complexity, it also means that they will tend to develop practices that actively utilize the many apps and devices and the many communication options within apps and adopt new apps and devices as they become available. Over time, these successful practices of connection may deepen the embedding of communication technology within personal networks.

But what exactly are the mediated communication practices that exist within complex social and technological configurations? While it may be possible to make theoretical speculations about these practices of connection, they are better understood through empirical study. Such a study is the focus of Part II.

PART II

Practices of Connection

5

Discovering Practices of Connection

In Part I, I argued that the social implications of constant connectivity are evident in our practices of connection. Practices of connection are reoccurring communicative actions that typically involve communication technology. As such, they are the means by which technology and social life become mutually embedded. The configuration approach suggests that social complexity and technological complexity have coevolved through a social ecological selection of communication practices. These communication practices survive to the extent that they are consistent with complex social and technological configurations. This leads to a new question: What are the practices of connection that stem from and perpetuate social and technical complexity?

Knowledge of specific types of communication practices that exist in the world cannot be confidently gained through a priori inferences and speculation. An empirical approach is needed to gather evidence that can help us to accurately identify communication practices and the configurations that influence them. In this chapter, I will discuss a study that I developed and led to understand these social practices and configurations using a mix of quantitative and qualitative data. The results of this study are the basis of claims made in the remainder of this book.

This study is unique in the multimethod approach that it uses to combine digital trace, survey, and in-depth interview data collected in Canada during a five-year period, from 2017 to 2022. There has been

---

The Digital Bind. Jeffrey Boase, Oxford University Press. © Oxford University Press (2025).
DOI: 10.1093/oso/9780197798591.003.0006

a great deal of interest in digital trace data among social scientists over the previous two decades, yet there are still many theoretical, ethical, and methodological challenges to collecting and making sense of this data. In this chapter, I will explore several challenges and how this study addresses them. It is my hope that this study might serve as an example of how researchers can address some of these challenges and overcome at least some limitations of digital trace data by tightly integrating it with more traditional survey and interview methods. Understanding the nature of this study is also critical to understanding the results that are discussed in the next three chapters.

A MULTIMETHOD APPROACH TO UNDERSTANDING PRACTICES OF CONNECTION

In this section, I discuss the methods that I used in the study and how I wove digital trace data into my research design. The use of digital methods is fitting for collecting data on communication practices, which are often difficult to accurately understand through self-reports and collect ethically. Nevertheless, as I argue in Chapter 3, personal network complexity implies the reflexive understanding, articulation, and perhaps creation of social rules that underlie communication practices. Reflexivity is a subjective process, so it is not easily understood using digital methods that are optimized to capture behavior. Therefore, in addition to drawing on digital methods to understand communication behavior, I also use a qualitative method that will collect rich insights into the reflexive meaning-making process underlying communication practices.

Moreover, the theory that I have drawn on leads me to expect that personal network complexity is prevalent throughout many contemporary societies, particularly in those with knowledge- and service-based economies. Such universality demands a method that allows for the production of generalizable knowledge claims at a societal level. Generalizable claims require a large and random sample drawn from a population, which will be quantitative in nature. In short, although digital methods are useful for understanding behavior, my theoretical interests also require more traditional qualitative and quantitative methods. How can all these methods be combined?

When approaching this study, I wanted to leverage the strengths of digital and traditional qualitative and quantitative methods. Research methods are ultimately epistemological tools, in that they are approaches to acquiring new knowledge about the world. The tool metaphor implies that different tools are designed for different tasks. No single tool is designed for all epistemological tasks, meaning no single method will allow researchers to acquire all types of knowledge. In this way, each research method has strengths and limitations. A strength of survey methods is the ability to generalize to larger populations. However, surveys cannot produce a rich understanding of subjective meaning similar to that of in-depth interviews. By the same token, in-depth interviews are time-consuming and are not typically conducted to generalize findings to populations. A limitation of both surveys and interviews is that although respondents can self-report their behaviors, these self-reports can lack richness, and it's difficult to feel confident that they represent real behavior.

A FLEXIBLE APP FOR THE ETHICAL COLLECTION OF DIGITAL TRACES

Digital trace data were collected using a mobile phone app that I designed with a former PhD student, Junji Zhe, MA student Yingduo Tang, and visiting student Hirokazu Oda. This app collects data from a population-level survey, in-depth interviews, and the ethical collection of digital traces (during both the survey and interview). Before discussing this app, a general discussion of the ethical issues surrounding the use of digital trace data may be of interest to some readers. So as not to distract from the topic at hand, I have placed this discussion in the appendix.

As opposed to most commercial apps, the app developed for this study was specifically created to be a research tool. Although the app could be installed by anyone using a phone with Google's Android operating system, a participant ID was required to use the app. Participant IDs were given only to those who were asked to participate in the survey and interviews. After entry of a participant ID, the app provides a clear and detailed explanation of what data it would collect, how and why it was being collected, and other information about the nature of the questions being asked in the survey or interviews. Respondents recruited into the survey were also provided with an explanation of the data collection through materials included in a mailed invitation. Those being interviewed were provided with paper-based and verbal explanations by the interviewers. Once a respondent read the explanation provided through the app and agreed to continue participating, the app collected data from the call and text logs stored on the device. They included the times and dates of calls and text messages, if a call or text was incoming or outgoing (i.e., made/received, sent/received), the duration of each call, the number of characters of each text, and the time zone in which the phone was located.

The app did not collect phone numbers, names, or the content of text messages. This information was not necessary to answer my research questions, and avoiding its collection reduced the possibility of deanonymization. However, to know if respondents were calling or texting the same phone numbers or different ones, the app created a random string of numbers and digits that represented each phone number. This way, if a respondent was calling or texting the same phone number several times, we could understand the frequency of communication with this relationship without collecting the name or phone number of the participant or the person with whom they were communicating. The area code of the phone number was retained as the first three digits of the longer identifier, allowing us to know if they were communicating with people who were local (sharing the same area code) or more geographically dispersed.

Given that individuals sometimes have more than one phone number—such as when they use a personal mobile phone and a work phone—the app also created a random number that represented the contact in the address book associated with each phone number. This meant that if there were two phone numbers located under the same name in the phone's address book, the app would assign the same random number to both phone numbers. This allowed me to know if there was communication with the same individual using multiple devices. The names in the address book and the actual phone numbers were not recorded in this process. Moreover, all the processing of these phone numbers and names to strip them of information was done on the respondent's device and never uploaded to a server or other device.

After the app had completed the processing and stripping of the digital trace data located in the respondent's call and text logs, it asked on-screen questions. In the case of the survey, these questions were how respondents completed the survey. In the case of the interviews, these questions were asked during the interviews at specific points. More than simply administration of on-screen questions, one of the most unique aspects of this app was that it allowed for the integration of these questions with digital trace data. As mentioned in the previous section, digital trace data often lack context. In this project, I am interested in understanding not only the behavioral sides of communication practices but also the nature of the relationships in which they occur. Given my focus on the role of family and work institutions, I wanted to understand the social role of the individuals with whom respondents communicated. My interest in these relationships related to tie strength, meaning that I wanted to understand the closeness of these relationships. Finally, I wanted to understand the reflexive meanings that respondents gave to their communication practices with these relationships.

To "fill out" the contextually weak digital trace data, this app asked on-screen questions and associated them with identifiers that represented the phone numbers of contacts. To do this, a question could ask, "Please select someone that you work with from your address book or call log." The respondent could then locate this individual in their address book or call log (Figure 5.1). Once this individual was selected, the app would

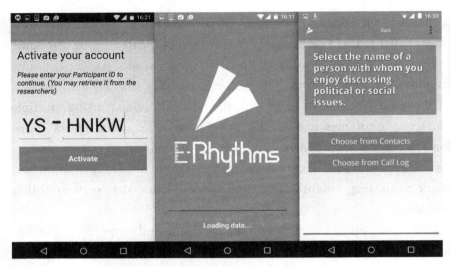

Figure 5.1. Three screenshots taken from the data collection app. Account activation (left), app logo (middle), and a survey question (right).

record the identifier associated with this individual's phone number(s). The app could then follow up with other on-screen questions, in which the respondent could indicate how close they felt to this person or the specific nature of their relationships at work (e.g., manager or coworker). A similar approach was used during interviews, in which the interviewer would ask a respondent to use the app to select someone they work with, followed by in-depth questions about their communication practices with them. This approach allowed for associating contextual information with the behavioral information obtained through digital traces.

Although the app allowed for the informed, consensual, and integrative collection of digital trace data, it was not without its limits. Most obviously, there are many other ways that individuals communicate other than mobile calls and texts; digital traces of these communications were not collected. For example, communication occurring through social media apps was not collected. The reason for this was simple: at the time, almost all social media platforms did not allow independently developed apps to access communication data. Most companies profited from the collection and use of these data, so it was typically not in their interests to make them accessible to others.

Fortunately, although social media messaging apps have exploded in popularity, at the time of data collection in Canada, most individuals still used their default texting apps. The results of the national survey that I will discuss in more detail in the next section showed that 46% of the respondents reported using their default texting app more frequently than other messaging apps. Facebook Messenger was the second most common app for sending messages (approximately 19% of respondents reported using it the most to send messages). Yet those mostly using Facebook Messenger still exchanged on average the same number of messages using the default texting app as those who reported mostly using the default texting app. In other words, even those who reported using Facebook Messenger more often than other messaging apps still used the default texting app just as much as those who reported using the default texting app more than other apps. In contrast, the 17% of respondents who reported using WhatsApp the most to send messages sent on average about half the number of messages using the default texting app than respondents who reported using the default texting app most often. This indicates that WhatsApp was partly used as a replacement for the default texting app.

Overall, these results indicate that default texting was still predominantly used by most of our respondents. This is possibly because the cost of texting became a standard part of most phone plans before other messaging apps became widely available. In contrast, countries in which social media messaging apps were quickly adopted en masse more often required that individuals pay for each text message sent via the default texting app.

In sum, the app was developed as a means of collecting digital traces and integrating them into more traditional survey and interview methods. This integration provides a more complete understanding of communication behavior by using traditional methods to better understand the contextual nature of digital traces, such as relational roles of contacts. Although it is not possible to ethically collect digital traces produced by communication media, the development of this app is a first step toward having a more accurate and holistic understanding of mediated communication practices.

PRACTICES OF CONNECTION AND THE CHALLENGE OF GENERALIZATION

A lengthy philosophical argument about the possibility of generalization in social research would not bring us any closer to addressing questions about the connection between practices of connection, complexity, and constant connectivity. I believe a more fruitful route is to consider the generalizations necessary to address these questions as they arise in the context of the theoretical arguments that I presented in previous chapters. To that end, I have drawn on social theory to generalize about personal network complexity and the complexity of technology in everyday social life. I have already made the case that the ethical collection of digital trace data can help produce an empirically based understanding of complex social behavior. However, it is also important to consider the populations in which complex behaviors occur.

To develop an understanding of practices of connection that draws on evidence rather than a priori reasoning, it is necessary to discover and collect evidence in a way that generalizes findings to large populations. This requires considering which countries or populations I want to research empirically. For this study, I was fortunate enough to receive funding from the Social Science and Humanities Research Council (SSHRC) of Canada. While this funding was substantial, it was not enough to fund the collection of data from multiple countries, nor did I have the many collaborators or research infrastructure necessary to accomplish such a study.

Due to these practical considerations, I decided to focus on Canadian society. Canada is an ideal setting in which to find the type of personal network complexity discussed in Chapter 3. The social institutions of work and family have been changing and becoming more complex in Canada over the previous decades. Divorce is relatively common, and the birth rate has decreased. People are getting married later in life (or not at all), as nontraditional cohabitation arrangements and same-sex unions have increased (Wu and Schimmele 2011). Moreover, Canada is very much a knowledge- and service-based economy in which many individuals change jobs and careers numerous times during their adult lives (Statistics Canada 2021).

Having chosen to collect data in Canada, I was further faced with the task of creating generalizations about the mediated communication practices of its approximately 38 million inhabitants. When social researchers wish to collect empirical evidence that allows for generalizations about large populations, they often use survey methods. As mentioned, the app developed for this project was designed to administer an on-screen survey that added context to those digital traces. But how was I to recruit a set of individuals living in Canada to install this app and complete an on-screen survey?

The ability to recruit a large set of individuals to complete the survey is critical to the generalizability of the resulting data. But what is often overlooked is the importance of recruiting a set of people that represent the population as a whole. Without representativeness, it is possible to have an extremely large sample that does not reflect the diversity of an entire population. This often happens when researchers recruit participants using a method that naturally selects only a certain type of individual. A prime example is when companies create panels of individuals by posting advertisements on websites such as job recruiting websites. This approach naturally excludes most people in a population who are not looking for employment and who do not have reliable internet access. It also creates other kinds of systematic sampling biases. For example, individuals that rely on job recruiting websites tend to be less socially connected and have lower levels of education than those who have found jobs through personal connections or who are more actively recruited by companies looking for their expertise.

One of the best ways to ensure that a sample of individuals represents a whole population is to randomly recruit individuals within that population to participate. The challenge to this approach is that to randomly ask people, you must first have a complete list of people that you could ask, along with their contact information. Obviously, I did not have such a list for everyone living in Canada. One common way researchers surmount this barrier is to hire research companies to administer telephone surveys. However, given that response rates to phone surveys have dropped in the past two decades—along with other issues created by the fact that individuals sometimes have both mobile phones and landline phones—this approach is now unreliable. Moreover, given that this project was designed to administer a survey on a mobile app, asking people to install an app on their phones while at the same time speaking to them over their phones is not practical.

Another common recruiting method is to select a set of people from a larger panel of individuals who have already agreed to do surveys. People are often recruited into survey panels by research companies, who then charge researchers a fee for administering surveys to their panel participants. While this approach is often the only cost-effective way researchers can recruit people to complete their surveys, it too can have serious methodological shortcomings. While it may be possible to randomly ask people within panels to complete surveys, it is often unclear how they were recruited into panels. If the companies recruiting individuals into their panels do not use a method in which they are randomly asking people from a larger population to participate, the panels can be biased. While research companies often try to recruit individuals with similar demographic traits as a larger population into their panels, selection bias can still emerge. For example, if a research company targets people who are looking for employment, offering them money for completing surveys will result in a set of individuals very unlike the overall population in certain ways.

When deciding how to approach recruiting for my app survey, a postdoctoral researcher working with me on this project, Dr. Guang-Ying Mo, contacted every research company that she could find located in Canada and asked them for details on how they recruited participants into their panels. No company was willing to provide a clear and detailed account of their recruiting methods. Many of these companies did say that the sample they could provide from their larger panels would be demographically like the Canadian population. However, given that mediated communication practices may not align perfectly with demographic traits, we were concerned about the possibility that the selection of individuals into these panels would bias results.

Given my concerns about recruiting by phone or using a panel, I decided to approach recruiting using a different method. I discovered that my university's library had purchased a database containing 9.7 million addresses located within Canada, 6.1 million of which were residential. A PhD student working on this project, Jack Jamieson, was able to merge another database of postal codes in Canada, which allowed us to assess the extent to which these addresses might over- or underrepresent geographic areas within Canada. Overall, there was no evidence of systematic bias in the location of the addresses, aside from a 7% oversampling of urban areas and 10% undersampling of rural areas.

The discovery of this address database enabled us to recruit participants by mail. Traditional mail survey methods have very low response rates, because respondents are required to complete a paper survey and return it through the post. By comparison, installing an app and completing a survey by phone requires less effort than a trip to a mailbox. Given the lack of alternatives, I decided to try sending recruiting materials by mail.

During the winter of 2017, my research team mailed invitations to 9,000 addresses randomly selected from my university's address database. The addresses were weighted such that selection adjusted for over- and underrepresentations of urban and rural addresses, respectively. We also excluded residents living in the French-speaking province of Quebec to avoid possible translation issues in the survey. The invitations included a letter that explained the nature of the project and how the app worked; a double-sided frequently asked questions (FAQ) sheet that explained in clear and simple language what data the app collected, why we were collecting it, and other more detailed information about the project; and finally, a page containing instructions on how to install the app and a unique identifier that respondents would need to enter after installing the app. This number could only be used once, to ensure that just one person per address installed the app. The materials also included information about optional compensation for completing the survey, which respondents could receive as an email money transfer, an Amazon gift card, or a gift card that could be used on a charity donation website.

In the end, a total of 410 individuals installed the app and completed the survey.[1] The log data from these respondents included digital traces of 1,874,224 text messages and 157,080 calls, totaling 2,031,304 calls and texts. As discussed in the previous section, these digital trace data included the date and time of each call and text, if it was incoming or outgoing, the area code of the phone numbers, the duration of each call, the length of each text, and phone numbers associated with address book contacts. The phone numbers, names, content of text messages, content of calls, and other recorded information were not collected.

Of our 9,000 invitations, 823 (0.01%) were returned because the address no longer existed or contained errors, and 410 individuals installed the app and completed the survey. The completion rate was 4.7%.[2] However, it is also important to consider that not every invitation reached a resident who owned an Android phone, which was necessary to install the Android-based app. When taking into account that 35% of the Canadian population owned an Android phone at the time of the survey,[3] a more useful completion rate is estimated at approximately 13.4%. While this completion rate is relatively low, problems with representativeness always arise when those who decide not to participate are different from those who do participate in a way that biases the results of a study. This effect is known as systematic response bias, and I looked for evidence of this bias in two ways.

One way to detect systematic response bias is to see if a new sample differs from other, more reliable data. The Canadian census is known to be one of the most reliable sources of data on the Canadian population. Comparing these data to our sample does not show any marked differences in gender, education, working status, and age (see Table 5.1). However, overall, those who installed the app and completed the survey were somewhat younger (thirty-three years on the app survey versus forty years in the census) and more likely to have a university degree. It is not surprising that those who installed the app and completed the survey were somewhat younger and more educated than the general population. People who owned smartphones, had the data plans necessary to download apps, and were technically competent enough to find an app and install it tended to be younger and more educated. Nevertheless, these differences were not extreme, which bodes well for the generalizability of this sample.

While demographics are useful indicators of systemic response bias, bias can also show up in other ways. Ultimately, the bias that presents the greatest problems for generalizability is that which influences

Discovering Practices of Connection   107

Table 5.1. DEMOGRAPHIC TRAITS OF PARTICIPANTS WHO COMPLETED THE APP
AND ONLINE SURVEYS, AND THE CANADIAN NATIONAL CENSUS

		App survey	Online survey	Census
Gender (%)	Male	52	51	50
	Female	48	49	50
	Fluid or nonbinary	0.01	0	Not asked
Education (%)	Less than high school	4	5	15
	High school diploma	23	15	27
	Vocational diploma	27	27	30
	Undergraduate degree	27	30	20
	Postgraduate degree	19	23	6
Working Status (%)	Unemployed/not working	9	6	NA
	Retired	7	15	NA
	Full-time student	18	12	NA
	Employed	66	67	67
Age	Median	33	43	46
	Mean	37	44	47

how people respond to survey questions. For example, it is possible that
people who were comfortable installing a data collection app on their
phones were more trusting than those who were not. Higher levels of
trust could mean that these people, in general, were more likely to install and use other kinds of apps, such as social media apps, from which
data were also collected. Ultimately, this effect might influence how respondents answered questions about their social media use or the kinds
of apps they used on their phones. Another related issue could arise if
Android phone users answered survey questions differently than iPhone
(or other types of phone) users.

To gain a better sense of how the willingness or ability to install an
Android-based app might have created a response bias, I worked with
my team to recruit another group of 111 respondents. These respondents
were also recruited through mailed invitations, and they completed a
survey that was nearly identical to the app-based survey. However, this

group was asked to complete an online survey rather than install a mobile app. The only difference between the online survey and the app survey was that the app survey asked respondents to select certain individuals, such as a very close friend, from their address books or phone logs. The web survey only asked respondents to think of these same types of individuals.

After both the app and online surveys were completed, I ran statistical comparisons of every question in both surveys. Of the 163 variables generated by the answers to the survey questions, only 10 showed statistical differences.[4] Statistical differences were unlikely to be the result of chance alone. A closer inspection of these variables showed only one variable with differences that seemed to be substantially significant: age. Respondents who completed the online survey were an average of seven years older (forty-four years old) than those who installed the app survey (thirty-seven years old). When considering the similar responses to the many other questions in the survey, this age difference does not imply that those who installed the app were more likely to answer survey questions significantly differently than those who decided not to install it.

Ultimately, it would have been even closer to ideal to collect one more sample, in which respondents completed a paper-based survey. Responses from a paper-based survey would help us better understand if there was response bias between those who completed an app or web survey and those who may not have the means, comfort level, or technological skill required to complete these types of surveys. However, as with all research projects, there is a balance between what is ideal and what is feasible. Given the low response rates to mail-based paper surveys, I decided that attempting to collect paper survey results was not viable.

To compensate for the fact that app users tended to be younger and more educated in the app and online surveys than in the census, I used the census results to create a "weight variable," which I applied to my analyses used in this book. This variable influenced the results of my analyses based on age and education, such that underrepresented groups were given more weight in the analysis.

Overall, the comparison with census results and the online survey indicates that the results of app surveys can be safely generalized to the adult population. But to what degree can we be confident that the results of the 410 individuals who installed the app survey, and the 111 respondents who completed the online survey, can be accurately generalized to the larger population?

With any random sample, it is possible that purely by chance, the people who are drawn from the population are in some ways different from the rest of the population. The larger the sample, the lower the probability that the individuals selected are different from the rest of the population. When presenting the results that come from the two identical surveys, I group answers from the 410 app respondents with the 111 online survey respondents to increase the total sample size. Using standard statistical calculation, with these 521 respondents, we can be 95% confident that the results reflect the true values in the adult Canadian population by plus or minus 4%.[5] For example, if the results of the surveys show that 79% of respondents learn about social issues from social media at least once a week, this means that we can be 95% confident that the actual percentage of adults learning about social issues at least once a week is between 75% and 83%. When using only results from the 410 respondents that completed the app survey, we can be 90% confident about the generalizability of the results at this same 4% margin of error.

In sum, producing generalizations about communication practices is challenging and requires novel approaches to learning about the social world. By incorporating the mobile data collection app into a new approach to recruiting, I could generalize the results of the logged data and surveys at a societal level.

DISCOVERING PRACTICES AND REFLEXIVE UNDERSTANDINGS

Digital trace data can help us understand complex communication patterns that are not well captured through self-reports. National surveys can produce generalizations about communication patterns and how they relate to other contextual factors such as relational roles and jobs. However, neither of these approaches provides much insight into the reflexive process that individuals go through to make sense of their practices.

Moreover, while combining digital trace with contextual survey data may help to analyze certain calling and texting practices, they do not contain enough rich or insightful information to fully understand how these practices fit into other practices not captured by the available trace data. As already discussed, digital traces of other communication activities were not captured in this project, for a myriad of practical and ethical reasons. While the survey may capture indicators of these behaviors—such as whether a respondent viewed a social media post from a very close friend in the past week—that can be generalized to the broader population, this ultimately is not enough information to fully understand how this behavior is part of more complex communication practices.

To better understand reflexive communication practices, particularly to discover those not well captured through available calling and texting traces, I next draw on 110 semistructured, in-depth interviews conducted as part of this project. Semistructured interviews involve a set of questions that are not fully structured, meaning that interviewers can follow up with their own probing questions that they generate on the spot. This gives interviewers the flexibility to ask additional questions that help them to better understand interviewee responses and thereby gain a more in-depth understanding of the topics covered in the interviews. This depth of understanding is particularly important to generating insights on subjective understandings. Moreover, unlike a survey in which researchers have no opportunity to follow up on unexpected responses, semistructured interviews allow researchers to discover new things about participants and their lives that they may not have anticipated at the outset of the project.

These interviews were mainly conducted by students with me on this project. Through weekly meetings, we discussed their experiences during these interviews, and offered suggestions to help them improve their interviewing skills. I was impressed with how quickly they improved their skills and have found the results of these interviews to be incredibly insightful. It also became clear that many respondents felt comfortable interacting with students, perhaps in some cases more so than they would have with a university professor.

The 110 interviews were conducted from 2018 to 2022, with 52 occurring before the COVID-19 pandemic and the remainder occurring during the first two years of the pandemic. For the interviews conducted before the pandemic, respondents were recruited in public areas with high levels of foot traffic in the Greater Toronto Area. We targeted areas where individuals from a wide range of socioeconomic backgrounds would be walking, such as outside of central subway stations. Forty-two of the interviewees installed the data collection app on their phones. At points in the interview, they identified individuals in their address book or call log as part of their response to questions. The remainder of the interviews did not require the use of the app, which allowed us to capture a wider range of individuals who owned non-Android phones.

During the pandemic, we decided that rather than recruiting in public areas, students would recruit through their personal networks of friends and family. We ensured that the individuals who were asked to participate were not very close to the students conducting the interviews, so that they would not feel pressure to participate. We also attempted to recruit individuals from diverse socioeconomic and cultural backgrounds and of different age groups. In the end, the individuals who participated in the interviews were quite diverse, which helped me both to identify a wide range of subject understandings and communication practices and, at the same time, to feel more confident that the theme of the interviews reflected a reality that extended beyond a particular demographic group. During the interviews, we asked all of our questions regarding communication with their relationships with work, family, and friend ties before the pandemic. With each question, we followed up to see what had changed during the pandemic. The results discussed in this monograph are about life before the pandemic. While it would be interesting to consider how the pandemic changed communication, this is beyond the scope of this book.

CONCLUSION

Communication practices and their connection to social and technological complexity are not easily understood by any single method. By integrating digital, survey, and interview methods, I am able to provide a rich understanding of these phenomena. The next four chapters draw on the results of this study to reveal common practices of connection in the context of work, family, and friendship.

6

Three Common Practices of Connection

I will begin this chapter by providing a high-level overview of three practices of connection and discuss how they fit within the broader argument made in Part I. At the start of this book, I asked, What are the social implications of constant connectivity? Drawing on evidence from early and current mobile studies, I argued that both social and technological factors seem to influence the social implications of constant connectivity. I then provided a new theoretical framework called the configuration approach as a means of understanding how both social and technological factors influence the practices of connection. I theorized that practices of connection are enacted when individuals communicate with others and that commonly occurring practices of connection typically maintain and perpetuate complex social and technological configurations. Understanding these practices of connection and how they are enabled and constrained by complex social and technological configurations allows us to address our original question regarding the social implications of communication technology.

In the previous chapter, I discussed a unique multimethod study that I developed to uncover common practices of connection and understand how they fit within complex social and technological configurations. The results of this study show three common practices of connection: media situatedness, the division of media, and temporal boundaries. These

The Digital Bind. Jeffrey Boase, Oxford University Press. © Oxford University Press (2025).
DOI: 10.1093/oso/9780197798591.003.0007

results further show that power in the form of communicative autonomy intersects with these practices.

Media situatedness is a practice that occurs when individuals reflexively select communication media based on a variety of contextual factors. The communication media that they select from include the many mobile apps that enable voice, text, and video exchanges, as well as landline phone calls, computer-based communication apps, and in-person communication. Media situatedness arises as individuals navigate a variety of social situations in daily life where they must consider factors such as the purpose of their communication, their social role (and ambiguities surrounding their role), and the availability and media preferences of others.

The division of media refers to the practice of separating relationships into different media channels, within and between apps. For example, an individual might use one social media app (such as Facebook messenger) to communicate with friends from high school, another social media app to communicate with their colleagues, and another app to communicate with their inner circle of friends. Moreover, within one app they might have separate message threads that they use to communicate with family members, coworkers, and groups of friends. As with media situatedness, constant connectivity facilitates the division of media by enabling the constant potential of connection through a variety of media.

Temporal boundaries are the result of individual and collective practices that allow for the segmenting of time using communication media. These boundaries help individuals protect and manage their time so that they are not constantly being interrupted through digital media. They often rely on common understandings of when it is inappropriate to interrupt others using ephemeral media, such as voice or video calls, and when it is more appropriate to use artifact-based media, such as text or voice messages. Unlike media situatedness and the division of media, temporal boundaries are not facilitated by constant connectivity. Rather, they are practices that enable individuals to maintain a flow of activities in the face of constant connectivity.

Power is not itself a practice of connection, but it influences how practices of connection occur. In this study, I found that power in the form of communicative autonomy influences the extent to which individuals can effectively practice media situatedness and the division of media and enforce temporal boundaries. These findings show how social configurations can shape the social implications of constant connectivity in ways that are undesirable, unfair, and unjust.

Figure 6.1 provides a high-level overview of how common practices of connection fit within my broader argument. In the remainder of this chapter, I will discuss the main findings of my study as they relate to these practices of connection. I will first provide results establishing that respondents typically draw on many communication media in the presence of constant connectivity, as all three common practices of connection require these conditions.

COMPLEXITY AND CONSTANT CONNECTIVITY

As argued at the beginning of this book, mobile phones have become the primary means by which constant connectivity is realized for most of the population. The installation of multiple communication apps on smartphones has expanded the range of potential social interactions. The results of my study show that most smartphone users carry out many kinds of activities in their daily lives, using these complex devices in complex ways.

Given that the technological complexity of communication media has manifested most recently in the form of portable smartphones that enable the use of many different communication apps, it is useful to start with a basic understanding of how people use these devices. At the time of this study, 76% of Canadian adults owned a smartphone (Statistics Canada 2017a), and this number has continued to increase to the point where the complete ubiquity of smartphones within Canadian society is imminent. As discussed in Chapter 4, smartphones allow for the installation of software-based communication apps, and these apps have a high degree of technical complexity, providing individuals with numerous ways to communicate. The results of my app and online surveys show

Constant Connectivity

Constant connectivity has become part of life for much of the world's population.

What are the social implications of constant connectivity?

Mobile Studies

Mobile studies indicate that the social implications of constant connectivity are influenced by social and technological factors.

How do social and technological factors influence the social implications of constant connectivity?

The Configuration Approach

The social implications of constant connectivity arise as individuals draw on communication technology through their practices of connection.

Social and technological configurations are rules that enable and constrain practices of connection.

Social Configurations

Individuals reflexively draw on complex social rules to navigate personal networks.

Three dimensions of personal network complexity: institutional, relational, and temporal.

Technological Configurations

Algorithms, protocols, and hardware components draw on complex rules to run apps and devices.

Three dimensions of mediated communication complexity: variety of apps and devices, variety of communication options within apps, and the changing nature of apps and devices.

Three Common Practices of Connection

Media situatedness occurs when individuals reflexively select the most appropriate communication app and device for a given situation. Appropriateness is influenced by institutional, relational, and temporal factors.

The division of media is the separating of relationships into different media channels, within and between apps. This maintains separate social spheres within complex networks.

Temporal boundaries involve drawing on a variety of communication options to avoid interruption when managing complex personal networks.

Power influences the extent to which individuals have autonomy over these three practices of connection.

Figure 6.1. Argument structure as it relates to three common practices of connection.

Table 6.1. PERCENTAGE OF RESPONDENTS ENGAGING IN MOBILE ACTIVITY

Activity	%
Texting	96
Calling	96
Taking photos or videos	89
Emailing	87
Using social media apps	80
Checking the weather	74
Using maps apps	73
Reading the news	68
Watching videos	65
Playing games	56
Video chatting	25
Controlling their home	9
Other	9

that individuals take advantage of the many options available to them by using their phones for many kinds of activities, many of which are social in nature.

In the surveys, respondents were asked to indicate which of thirteen possible types of activities they do on their mobiles (see Table 6.1). On average, they used their mobiles to carry out eight different types of activities.[1] Somewhat surprisingly, the number of activities did not vary much by age or household education. In terms of age, the number of mobile activities did not vary much between the ages of eighteen and sixty-nine. It was only among respondents seventy years and older that mobile activities decreased by almost half. There are only minor differences in terms of household education, which is generally an indicator of socioeconomic status. Those with a college education or higher reported an average of close to nine activities, while those with less education reported an average of seven activities. Overall, complex mobile use is prevalent throughout the Canadian population, even though we might expect age or education to show more drastic differences in use. As I will argue in my discussion of temporal boundaries, inequalities manifest not so much in the complexity of mobile use but, rather, in the extent to which individuals have the relational power necessary to exert interpersonal control over this use.

It should be noted that almost all of the most common mobile activities were directly social in nature and included, texting, calling, emailing, and using social media apps. Many of the remaining activities may not be social at first glance, but they are often incorporated into social activities. For example, checking the weather and using maps apps could be done when traveling to see others in-person, photos and videos are often shared with others, and reading the news can provide material for future conversations. Moreover, while video chatting was not a common activity, internet speed and data constraints existing at the time of this research likely contributed to this finding. As speed increases and constraints loosen, it is quite possible that video chatting will be an increasingly common activity.

The use of mobiles as multicommunication media was a consistent theme throughout the interviews. Brady, a manager in his thirties, nicely encapsulated this common sentiment when asked how he uses his phone: "I use it as my primary source of communication with other people." Like many of those interviewed for this project, Brady draws on multiple communication apps, depending on those he is communicating with—for example, when he mentioned, "I recently deleted Viber just because all my friends switched to WhatsApp . . . . And then my mom and dad [and] I sometimes use email, or short texts. My mom uses SMS, WhatsApp, and email. My dad only uses email." This complex use of technology reflects a complex social reality in which different communication media are used in different social circumstances.

Having used the results of this study to establish that technological complexity manifests through the constant connectivity offered by mobiles, I will now discuss how this technological complexity is used in three common practices of connection.

Three Common Practices of Connection 119

MEDIA SITUATEDNESS

Institutional, relational, and temporal complexity mean that individuals often navigate many different social situations throughout the day. These situations often require that individuals reflexively choose which medium they will use based on several factors. A few of the many possible factors that influence medium selection within a particular situation are as follows:

- The purpose or nature of the communication.
- The schedule constraints of the individual(s) being contacted.
- The media preferences of the individual(s) being contacted.
- Idiosyncratic and historic patterns of media use with the individual(s) being contacted.
- General and often ambiguous expectations surrounding social roles.
- Cultural understandings of which medium is most appropriate given the nature of the situation.

These situations vary by the nature of the institution in which the relationship exists, the unique relational history of those with whom individuals communicate, and the temporal complexity arising from interacting with others who are on their own unique schedules. The more complex their social lives, the more unique situations there are in which they communicate. This can lead individuals to draw on a variety of media when communicating with work, family, and friend ties.

Drawing on different media within a single relationship has been termed "media multiplexity" by Caroline Haythornthwaite (2001), and she has found in her research that strong relationships tend to have greater media multiplexity than weaker ones (2005). I find some general support for this association between relational strength and media multiplexity. However, my results also show that it is not the strength of the relationships that directly drive media use but, rather, that individuals tend to be in a variety of situations with their closest relationships.

The greater the variety of social situations and social understandings existing within a relationship, the greater is the variety of media woven into that relationship.

It should be noted that while media selection within situations is typically reflexive, the larger process in which these choices are made may still include some habitual behavior. For example, on a commute home, a father may habitually glance at his mobile phone and notice a text message from his daughter. This message might be a request that he pick her up from her friend's house on his way home. In this situation, the father might have already chosen a route home that would make picking her up difficult. Given the time-sensitive nature of the request, he might reflexively decide to call his partner to see if she could more easily pick their daughter up. The choice to call rather than text his partner might be based on the knowledge that his partner does not often check her mobile phone for new text messages, so a call would more quickly get her attention. This example shows how an everyday situation can prompt reflexive media selection, even though knowledge of this situation arose through the habitual checking of a mobile device. Once the message is received, reflexive consideration regarding the time-sensitive nature of the situation and knowledge of his partner's mobile habits informed the father's media selection. Without the reflexive consideration of several factors in this situation, he may have chosen a medium that failed to bring about the desired outcome. While it is true that individuals may sometimes select media through habit, the larger point being made is that if individuals always habitually select media, it would be difficult if not impossible for most people to successfully manage the flow of social interactions that are part of contemporary social life. This general tendency to select different media based on reflexive consideration of factors that are unique to a variety of situations is evident in the results of this study.

In the national survey developed for this study, respondents were asked to think about particular relationships, including a very close friend, somewhat close friend, someone from work, and someone they live with. They were then asked to identify the various media that they used in the past week to connect with each of these relationships.

Of the ten possible media listed,[2] respondents indicated that they used an average of approximately three media in the past week to connect with a very close friend, two media to connect with a somewhat close friend, three media to connect with a work tie, and a three to connect with a home tie. In terms of the specific media used to connect with these various relationships, respondents reported many different combinations. Eighty-seven unique media combinations were identified for very close friends, sixty-three for somewhat close friends, fifty-six for relationships at work, and sixty-five for relationships at home.[3] Overall, these findings show that a variety of media are used in a variety of relationships.

In-depth interviews conducted for this study help to explain why various media are used within specific relationships. As with the national surveys developed for this study, during the in-depth interviews, respondents were asked to think of particular relationships. However, instead of asking respondents to simply list all the media they used to connect with each of these relationships in the past week, respondents were asked to explain which media they typically used to connect with each relationship and why they would select these different media. In this process, respondents explained the social rules surrounding media use, how their technological properties allowed them to be used within the context of these rules, and how these social and technological configurations related to particular types of social situations. In the three chapters that follow, I will explore the connection between these social and technological configurations, and how they relate to situations that arise within the context of work, home, and friend relationships.

THE DIVISION OF MEDIA

In addition to asking respondents if they used social media apps on their phones, the surveys asked them to report on which, if any, of thirteen specific social media platforms they have used in the past month. Only 5% of the respondents reported not using any social media platforms in the past month.[4] On average, respondents reported using an average of three social media platforms,[5] and 74% report using at least two social media platforms in the past month. The most commonly used platform is Facebook (used by 80% of the respondents), followed by Instagram (41%) and Twitter (27%).

The in-depth interviews provide some context for the diversity of platforms used and why certain platforms, such as Facebook, are still commonly used at this time. Many respondents explained that they used this platform to maintain a sense of awareness about relationships that they no longer see in-person, even if they are not actively posting to the platform themselves. Zack, a medical specialist in his thirties, explained his connections on Facebook as follows:

> Former work colleagues, typically will be Facebook friends . . . . It's mostly me seeing what they do because I don't really do anything on Facebook. And then, you know, there's more, there's even more peripheral people, like friends of my girlfriend's . . . relatives, of course, as well. Some relatives I don't speak to on a frequent basis. So, they often use Facebook as a platform to post pictures of their kids, you know, just the general goings on and all that sort of stuff . . . then maybe some other friends who I've met through gaming and stuff like that in my past, but you know, we no longer game together, but we're still, have a peripheral relationship.

The embedding of popular social media platforms into social life through the continual enactment of particular social practices is evident here. For many, these practices involve visiting the platform as a way of maintaining awareness of the lives of social ties, particularly ties with whom there is little or no contact. These are often ties with whom there was active communication in the past, often through activities at work, through families, or at previous schools. The lack of shared activities in work or family arrangements implies a set of social configurations that are not conducive to active communication, even though there may still be interest in maintaining some sense of connection. As argued by Keith Hampton (2016), commonly used social media platforms can provide individuals with a means of persistent contact and pervasive awareness that might be difficult to maintain without these technological means.

In the broader context of institutional arrangements, individuals may move between several different work and family arrangements throughout their lives, and maintaining some sense of connection—or at least the potential for connection—with these less active social ties can still be advantageous. These relationships can help individuals connect with important information that could help them find a job, or perhaps they may provide support that would help them work through a family crisis. Within this broader social context, individuals have developed practices to passively use popular social media platforms, if only because this is the only means by which they can maintain some awareness of their weaker social connections. At different times and places, different social media platforms may fill this function. The point is not that there is anything intrinsic to a platform such as Facebook that explains its role as a means by which weak relationships are monitored and minimally maintained. Rather, there is a networked effect whereby the value of the platform for most users comes from its large user base; if they are going to find, monitor, and potentially reconnect with inactive relationships, they are most likely to find them on these platforms due simply to their popularity.

While certain social media platforms provide a means of persistent and pervasive awareness, more insightful to my argument regarding technological complexity is the great diversity of platforms respondents had used in the past month. Although Facebook was the mostly commonly used platform, only 14% of the respondents reported using only Facebook. Of the 13 possible social media platforms we asked about, 511 respondents used 237 unique combinations of social media platforms. For example, the most common combination of using Facebook, Instagram, and LinkedIn was reported by only 4% of the respondents. These results indicate that most respondents draw on several social media platforms and that there is no widely prevalent combination of social media platforms. In short, while certain platforms may be more commonly used than others, the combination of social media platforms that individuals use is highly diverse and indicates a high level of idiosyncratic social media use among respondents.

Why do individuals tend to draw on unique combinations of social media platforms? Put differently, why isn't it the case that most people simply use one social media platform? The interviews indicate that individuals tend to use different platforms to communicate with different people in their personal networks and that they tend to use specific functions within these platforms for certain activities. Melissa, a librarian in her thirties explained,

> Facebook is for family and friends and some like neighborhood acquaintances. Instagram is a mixed bag. I have coworkers on Instagram, I have friends on Instagram, even businesses and things I find interesting I follow on Instagram. Twitter is mostly business; I don't really use Twitter for social things. Snapchat is fun. I mostly use it for family and my one close friend. Like I have one close friend that we snapchat each other back and forth. My mom likes Snapchat, so she always sends funny pictures. I don't know if she got into it because of the filters. She likes me to send pictures of the kids, so they like it and use the filters too.

The complex ways in which people combine and use social media platforms means that Melissa's use of these platforms is somewhat unique. But it reflects a general theme in the interviews, which is the use of particular platforms for particular kinds of interactions or more socially passive activities. For example, although Melissa did not mention that she uses social media to join certain groups, some respondents explained that they only use platforms such as Facebook to participate in local groups. By joining groups within social media platforms, individuals learn about events and activities in their neighborhoods or condo buildings. Others still only use specific platforms for business purposes. Nina, a nurse who also is also a business owner explained,

> I'm a 42-year-old woman. I barely know how to post. I actually pay someone to do my social media because I do medical aesthetics on the side. I have a small business, and I do injections like Botox

filler, and so I pay someone to do my social media because . . . I know I could learn, but I just don't want to.

There are many other examples of these types of niche uses of specific functions with social media platforms throughout the interviews.

In sum, the combined results of the national surveys and interviews show that individuals draw on communication technology in complex and often individualistic ways. They use the many communication channels available to them on their mobile devices to connect with different types of relationships and to carry out different types of social activities. This complex technological use is indicative of complex social configurations in which individuals actively choose from many communication options depending on their specific relationships and social situations. While there are some common uses of certain communication channels—such as using popular social media platforms to maintain a sense of connection with former friends, colleagues, and infrequently contacted family members—the diverse ways that individuals draw on other social media and other communication apps through their mobile devices reflects the complex nature of social life.

TEMPORAL BOUNDARIES

In the past, temporal boundaries could be maintained through spatial separation. Work and home typically existed in separate locations, and these physical boundaries created temporal boundaries in which availability was often limited at certain times of the day. Temporal boundaries also occurred during times of transit. However, mobile devices lowered the role that spatial separation could play in creating temporal boundaries.

How do individuals manage the potential of constant connectivity without constant interruption? While this may appear to be an individual problem, a recurring theme from the interviews is that temporal boundaries are often collectively understood.

They are often maintained through implicit and explicit social rules about when it is appropriate to use media that require the immediate attention of others, versus those that do not. These rules are sometimes based on the individual's social role within institutions, such as when a father feels that it is appropriate to call his children any time they are away from the home, while at the same time feeling it is better to email colleagues so as not to interrupt them. These decisions about what medium to use are also situationally based, and social rules and personal knowledge are applied accordingly. For example, while it might generally be appropriate to email a colleague, in situations requiring their immediate response it may also be appropriate to call them. The social configurations that allow individuals to maintain temporal boundaries are complex insofar as they vary considerably depending on the unique combinations of role, knowledge of the other, and situational context.

The process of acquiring this knowledge about when it is appropriate to use a particular medium is not always formally taught, and more often learned through trial and error. This came up several time in the interviews for this project, and is well captured by Joyce, who is piano teacher in her 50s:

> I find nowadays when you just call people, they seem surprised. They say, "why are you trying to call me". I had an experience where I tried to call an old friend. She lives in England, and we haven't talked in a long time. So, when I called her the first thing she said was "why did you call me?" It sounds like for every call I need to make a schedule, which is pretty weird to me. But I got used to it now. It feels like intruding into someone's life when you just call .... The first I found this out was when teaching I tried to call a student about scheduling, but he expected me to text . . . that was like 10 years ago. That was when I realized the world has changed to texting instead of calling.

The technological configurations required to maintain these boundaries are also complex in that they provide a wide range of media options, each of which may be appropriate depending on the nature of their

Three Common Practices of Connection

role, knowledge of the other, and the situation. As I will show in the remaining chapters, having many technological options does not boil down simply to breaking a temporal boundary with a call versus maintaining the boundary with a text. There are many other options, such as the use of several different texting apps, the use of threaded group conversations within messaging apps, the leaving of text-based voice message, and video calling, to name a few. Nevertheless, despite the technological complexity of these various options, their usage as it relates to temporal boundaries suggests a natural grouping based on the distinction made in Chapter 4 between digital artifact-based and ephemeral media. Ephemeral communication media—typically, voice or video calls—require that communication occurs immediately, which makes conducting concurrent activities challenging or impossible. In contrast, artifact-based communication media—such as texting/messaging, email, social media posts, voice messages, and so on—are not configured such that they require the immediate attention of two or more individuals.[6]

A reoccurring and widely prevalent theme in the 110 interviews conducted for this study shows that respondents tend to use digital artifact-based media in a variety of situations and reserve ephemeral media for time-sensitive situations, emergencies, or when they feel the people that they are contacting ought to be available to communicate with them. While there may be some exceptions to these general trends, the division of media into those media that will not interrupt the activities of those being contacted versus those media that will interrupt people is often a key consideration when selecting a particular medium. This logic was well captured by Jason when he explained why he communicates using WhatsApp:

Uh, quite important to my life now, like it's the main . . . the most important or like most popular communication tools that I'm using, right. Yeah. Compared to talking on the phone . . . . If I message them on WhatsApp, right, they don't have to read it right away. They can read it later on; they can reply to it later on. They don't even have to type anything, my parents; they can just like, record a message, right? By using voice function, right.

It should be noted that while WhatsApp allows for the exchange of text messages, several respondents indicated that they also use it for the exchange of voice messages, and sometimes voice or video-based calls. Several media are contained within this one app. In Jason's quote, it is apparent that among these options for communication, artifact-based text or voice messages are more desirable than an ephemeral call mainly because they do not require his parents to stop the flow of their activities. Moreover, they have some choice in how they respond—choosing either to type a text-based message or leave a voice message. With either option, their response will be an artifact, and Jason will himself have some flexibility in how and when he responds.

Although social rules result in the collective maintenance of temporal boundaries, individuals can also act reflexively in ways that help them to maintain their own personal temporal boundaries. The complex configuration of mobile devices allows users to silence all incoming communications or selectively allow only notifications from certain individuals. Individuals also act reflexively in ways that draw on personal knowledge of the people they might want to contact and to make decisions about the most appropriate medium for maintaining the temporary boundaries of these individuals. In these cases, they may be drawing not on widely held social rules of which technology to use but, rather, on particular knowledge about those they are contacting. This is true particularly in close relationships, where there is knowledge of the other person's schedule and media preferences. My study shows that individuals often reflexively decide when to use their unique knowledge of the individual they are contacting versus following norms of appropriateness on a case-by-case basis.

Temporal boundaries are also individually determined when there is tension or emotional distance between relationships. In this case, ephemeral media may be avoided simply because they require more acute and psychological engagement than artifact-based communication, and artifact-based media become the desired means of communicating. However, given that the use of artifact-based media tends to be consistent with the general trend toward maintaining temporal boundaries, this type of motivation may not be apparent to others or even to the person that is being avoided. The larger point being made is

Three Common Practices of Connection

129

that while social rules influence media selection, unique relational histories also play a role, particularly when they are consistent with rules that support the maintenance of temporal boundaries.

In the remaining chapters, I will show the various ways in which individuals use mediated communication practices to maintain temporal boundaries given complex social and technological configurations.

POWER AND PRACTICES OF CONNECTION

While constant connectivity itself is not intrinsically beneficial or detrimental, when it exists in the context of unequal social configurations, individuals can lack autonomy over these common practices of connection. This occurs when individuals are not allowed to exercise control over their use of communication media, which makes it difficult or impossible to effectively practice media situatedness, a division of media, and temporal boundaries. This lack of power is often the result of institutional inequalities.

Within specific relationships, undesirable situations often arise when an individual lacks institutional power. This often occurs in formal work environments when workers lack the autonomy to refuse ephemeral communications. For example, Anika, who works as an administrative support person in a traditional office at a large company, prefers to keep her phone in her purse. However, she is not given that choice

> because my manager expects me to uh, like she wants to be in touch with me . . . . So that's why I'm keeping my phone on my desk, otherwise previously I was not even keeping it on my desk. . . . But now she's expecting, and now you have that thing in front of you, so you will see it.

Referring to her phone as "that thing," Anika is clearly unhappy about being constantly available to her manager and the technology that enables this availability. Even though this phone is her personal property, she lacks full control over it when at work. This example illustrates how larger institutional configurations and inequalities within social roles can coincide with technologically enabled availability to create undesirable situations.

Situations in which respondents felt obligated to use various media against their own preferences existed in other ways as well. Some respondents expressed concerns over the privacy implications of being on various social media platforms. Nevertheless, because others within their personal networks were active on these platforms, they felt the need to use them, at least passively. Other respondents, often above fifty years of age, generally did not like being available all the time. Yet they still carried their mobile devices with them out of obligation to various family members or others who they felt would be upset if they were unable to contact them.

It is important to bear in mind that not all respondents disliked specific media, or technology more generally. Many respondents interviewed for this study seemed to take for granted that communication technology is part of their lives. While they generally had their own understandings of how, when, and with whom to use communication technology, this knowledge did not often evoke strong positive or negative sentiments. However, when the technologies became embedded into unequal social situations—that is, when they lacked control over common practices of connection—they tended to feel more negatively about them. The extent to which it becomes a problem for individuals often comes down to the extent to which they have the power and autonomy within their own unique work, family, and friendship arrangements to refuse undesirable interactions. The ability to control one's interactions is a critical aspect of institutional life before the development of constant connectivity. What is new is the ways in which this new technological possibility has woven itself into these social configurations and resulted in new undesirable practices.

CONCLUSION

The configuration approach helps us to understand that the social implications of constant connectivity can be found in the practices of connection that individuals employ when they communicate with others. Although these practices vary considerably from person to person, the configuration approach leads us to expect that common practices will emerge in large populations to the extent that they help to perpetuate and maintain common social and technological configurations.

As I argued in Chapters 3 and 4, social and technological complexity have increased over time. It is now common for individuals to maintain complex personal networks in which institutional arrangements are often shifting, relationships are actively constructed, and the temporal flow of interaction must be actively managed. At the same time, most individuals now have at their disposal a complex variety of communication apps and devices, many communication options within apps, and an ever-changing landscape of communication apps and devices. Given that these complex social and technological configurations are common in contemporary social life, we can expect that those practices of connection that are commonly adopted throughout the population will help to perpetuate and maintain the complexity of these configurations.

The results of my study show how the three common practices of connection discussed in this chapter all stem from and perpetuate complex social and technological configurations in the presence of constant connectivity. Media situatedness involves reflexive consideration of several contextual social factors. These factors vary from situation to situation because complex personal networks do not allow individuals to easily rely on a stable and widely shared set of social rules. Instead, the particularities of an individual's personal network will determine the most salient factors as they relate to the nature of the institutions, relationships, and temporal boundaries in which they are embedded. The complexity of communication media further means that individuals have a variety of medium options that they draw on in any given situation. As individuals draw on a variety of communication options within a variety of social situations, they are then both maintaining and perpetuating the social complexity of their personal networks and contributing to the continued complexity of communication media.

The division of media also stems from and perpetuates complex social and technological configurations. Personal network complexity means that individuals must actively construct their social roles by managing the flow of interactions that occur with the shifting institutions and relationships. Dividing relationships between many different apps, and threads within apps, helps to maintain and develop role complexity as people switch between and actively manage their various social roles.

Temporal boundaries stem from and perpetuate complex social and technological configurations by helping individuals to maintain complex personal networks without constant interruption. The variety of communication options available to individuals provides them with several ways of staying connected to various network members, many of which do not require synchronous communication. The exchange of text messages, pictures, videos, and voice messages provides the means of selecting a medium that is best suited to a particular situation without having to stop the flow of our own activities or the activities of the people with whom we are communicating. At the same time, when the timing is mutually convenient, there are also many options for more ephemeral communications, such as voice calling and video chats, through many different apps. In short, temporal boundaries facilitate the successful management of personal networks via the many communication options within and between apps.

Finally, it is important to understand that while these practices are common, power influences the ways in which they manifest. Those that lack the power to make autonomous decisions regarding when, how, and with whom they communicate will be limited in how they practice media situatedness, divide their media between relationships, and manage temporal boundaries. In effect, they may need to fit within practices of connection preferred by others that have power over them.

Returning to our overarching question, what do these results tell us about the social implications of constant connectivity? Constant connectivity is the foundation on which practices of connection exist. It has facilitated these practices to the point where they have become central to our social lives. While it is true that these practices could exist to some extent if we only relied on desktop computers and landline phones, they would be far more limited in scope. If this were the case, we could only practice them in particular locations, at particular times of day when

Three Common Practices of Connection   133

we were in those locations. Constant connectivity has meant that these practices are now a central and inescapable aspect of social life. In this way, they have embedded themselves fully into our lives, binding us to each other and to the complex technological apparatus that connects us.

Although media situatedness, the division of media, and temporal boundaries pervade the results of this study, they manifest in different ways within the context of work, family, and friendship. In the next three chapters I will draw on the results of my study to explore how these practices of connection occur in each of these contexts.

7

At Work

In this chapter, I draw on the results of my study to explore the social implications of constant connectivity in the context of work. I examine practices of connection across different types of occupations and consider how power influences the extent to which workers have control over these practices.

As discussed in Chapter 3, work institutions play an important role in structuring personal network complexity. In this chapter, I draw on sociological literature to argue that contemporary occupations often require that workers actively shape their social roles and act independently to maintain working relationships. This is particularly true of the knowledge- and service-based occupations that are central in many contemporary economies. In addition, I also discuss how power in the form of communicative autonomy is necessary if workers are to effectively shape their social roles at work and manage conflicting demands. Knowing how practices of connection manifest in different occupations and the role that power plays in these practices will deepen our understanding of the social implications of constant connectivity.

In the next section, I describe the results of the survey as they relate to the country of this study, Canada. In the sections that follows, I draw on the national survey results and in-depth interviews to explore practices of connection and power within the following four occupations: knowledge, service, public sector, and goods production.

The Digital Bind. Jeffrey Boase, Oxford University Press. © Oxford University Press (2025).
DOI: 10.1093/oso/9780197798591.003.0008

At Work 135

OCCUPATION IN A KNOWLEDGE AND SERVICE ECONOMY

Before proceeding, it is important to understand the various types of occupations that exist in Canada. Of the 521 individuals completing the national surveys, 378 (71%)[1] are employed in full-time or part-time jobs. All of these employed individuals are included in this analysis. The results show that 36% of workers are in knowledge occupations, 43% are in service occupations, 12% are in public sector occupations, and 9% are in goods producing occupations.[2]

The survey results also show how occupation is closely linked to wage (see Table 7.1).[3] Forty-one percent of the participants work in low-wage jobs, which are primarily in service and goods producing industries. In contrast, none of the respondents in knowledge or public sector organizations work in low wage jobs. The close mapping of occupational type and wage level is to be expected when considering that working in knowledge and public sector occupations generally requires higher levels of education and specialized knowledge than employment in service and goods producing occupations.

These results show that Canada is an ideal country in which to examine personal network complexity as it relates to knowledge- and service-oriented occupations. Although knowledge and service occupations are most common in Canada, small but significant percentages of Canadians work in the types of public sector and goods producing occupations that were more abundant in the mid-twentieth century.

Table 7.1. WAGE LEVEL BY OCCUPATION

	Knowledge occupation	Service occupation	Public sector occupation	Goods producing occupation	Total
Low wage (%)	0	77	0	81	41
Higher wage (%)	100	23	100	19	59

These occupations provide a natural comparison with which to examine the style of personal network complexity found in medium- and high-wage occupations and the lack of complexity in lower-wage occupations. Moreover, results pertaining to goods production may provide insight into practices that are more common in the global south and other parts of the world where goods production is more common. In short, while the results of this study are most generalizable to countries that are economically similar to Canada, the divisions of occupation into broad types helps provide some insights into other counties as well.

In this chapter, I will also consider how mediated communication practices manifest in all of these occupations and how these practices reflect various types of social complexity and power inequalities.

KNOWLEDGE OCCUPATIONS

Mohammed's story, which emerged during an hour-long in-depth interview, illustrates several common themes regarding social complexity and mediated communication practices in knowledge occupations.

Mohammed is a sales director at a large multinational company in Toronto, where he works regular hours in a traditional office environment. His job mostly involves leading a sales team, as well as developing and maintaining client relationships. His routine is structured around communication,

> 7 to 8 I finish all my emails. 8 to 8:30 I arrange my desk, because [my job] starts at 8:30. 8:30 to 9:30 I spend some time with my boss to see what's the plan for the day, and schedule our meetings and so on. 9:30 to 12 is all emails and responses. 12 to 1 is lunch, 1 to 4 I try to go out for sales calls, or prospective new business clients. 4 to 5:30 I spend with my team, to train them or help them with any of their requirements.

Mohammed's description of his day reveals several common tendencies found among knowledge workers in the population-level survey. First, it shows that although Mohammed works regular days of the week, he

At Work

Table 7.2. AUTONOMY AT WORK, WORKING AT HOME, AND WORK SCHEDULE BY OCCUPATION

	Survey question	Knowledge occupation	Service occupation	Public sector occupation	Goods producing occupation
Autonomy at work	Little/no freedom to make important decisions at work (%)	8	19	8	33
Work at home	Never work at home (%)	30	49	46	57
Work schedule	Work regular days of the week (%)	81	69	80	88
	Work regular hours (%)	91	87	98	86
	Often work outside of regular hours (%)	36	19	40	35
	No time off during winter holiday (%)	16	16	5	15

starts working an hour and a half before this day officially starts. As shown in Table 7.2, although 81% of knowledge workers work regular days of the week and 91% work regular hours, more than a third (36%) of them report working outside of regular hours. It is also clear from Mohammed's description that he exercises a fair degree of autonomy in this job when it comes to scheduling meetings, actively cultivating new client relationships, and training his team. The survey results show that autonomy to make important decisions at work is common among those working in knowledge occupations; only 8% say they have little or no freedom in this regard. Although Mohammed does not explicitly refer to working at home, given that he emails outside of his regular working hours, it would not be surprising if some of this communication occurred at home. 70% of the knowledge workers who completed the survey indicated that they work at home at least sometimes.

In short, like the majority of the knowledge workers surveyed, Mohammed's daily routine exhibits several dimensions of social complexity. Although his hours and days of work are regular, the importance of scheduling meetings and working outside of regular hours shows that temporal complexities must be constantly and reflexively managed. Active relational management with his clients is also a critical part of his job, as it is with his team too. All of these activities require a high degree of autonomy, which is also common among knowledge workers more broadly.

Turning to Mohammed's mediated communication practices, it is clear that these practices primarily involve heavy use of email, along with calling and in-person communication. Table 7.3 summarizes various patterns of media use that workers report for contacting someone they know from work in the past week. The most commonly used medium by knowledge workers is email, while texting is the most commonly used medium in other occupations. Considering the fundamental properties of commonly used media, it is clear that a majority of knowledge workers draw on artifact-based media (email and texting) in addition to ephemeral media (calling), while workers in other occupations most often draw on one type of artifact-based media (texting) and ephemeral media (calling). Of the two types of artifact-based media most commonly used by knowledge workers, email more easily allows for the exchange of detailed messages and documents that are optimized for computers. This indicates that knowledge workers are in social arrangements that are most conducive to communication that requires a mix of detailed informational artifacts, and shorter mobile text-based artifacts.

	Knowledge occupation		Service occupation		Public sector occupation		Goods producing occupation	
Average number of media used		2.6		2.5		2.5		1.6
5 most used media, excluding in-person communication (%)	Emailed	70	Texted	52	Texted	49	Texted	36
	Texted	49	Called	49	Called	46	Emailed	30
	Called	47	Emailed	27	Emailed	40	Called	18
	Read post(s)	12	Social media messaged	25	Social media messaged	24	Social media messaged	12
	Social media messaged	9	Read post(s)	23	Read post(s)	11	Read post(s)	2
3 most common media combinations, including in-person communication (%)	Emailed, texted, called and in-person	17	In-person only	16	Emailed, texted, called and in-person	11	In-person only	32
	Emailed and in-person	10	Texted, called and in-person	9	Emailed, texted and in-person	8	Emailed, texted, called and in-person	12
	In-person only	9	Texted and in-person	8	Texted and in-person	8	Texted and in-person	12

True to what might be expected in an office environment, Mohammed's communication at work mainly occurs through landline phones, email, and in-person conversations. When asked if he ever used his mobile at work he replied,

> 6 months back so I used to use it . . . . Because I was on social media and so many things, but 6 months back I made a conscious decision that it is taking too much of my time and my life. So, once I come to the office I try to avoid using my phone as much as possible, unless there are certain calls that I get which have different ringtones. So I know it's from my family or from a particular person so that I know it has to be an emergency.

This statement shows several mediated communication practices at work. Mohammed recognized that his mobile-based social media usage was at odds with his duties at work, so he reflexively decided to limit his use while at the office. Yet it is clear that he was also aware that the norms surrounding his obligations to his family or "a particular person" necessitated that he receive calls in the case of emergencies. To meet these expectations, he took advantage of the individualized configurations provided by his mobile to personalize his ringtones. Here, media situatedness is evident in Mohammed's decisions that help him to construct temporal boundaries as a way of managing constant connectivity. If any of these elements were missing—if his device did not allow for complex configuration, if his expectations at work or with family were differently configured, if he did not have a mobile that enabled the potential for constant connectivity, or if he lacked reflexivity—Mohammed's mobile use for both work and personal purposes could be quite different.

It would be enough to stop here, yet further discussion with Mohammed revealed an even more nuanced approach developing mediated communication practices in the context of complex social and technical configurations. When asked to explain his company's policy about mobile use Mohammed explained,

> Mobile phones are not allowed for personal usage during work hours, that is our HR policy. All our team members have

At Work 141

a landline, so I don't see any reason for anyone to use a mobile phone . . . . I have a mobile, it's not given by the company. But I have it because a lot of my connections I keep in touch with them on WhatsApp. Because [during] the last 7 years of my work, they have become my friends from clients. So that's the reason I got my mobile to the office, otherwise I wouldn't take my mobile to the office.

Then, after more discussion he elaborated,

Because a lot of my clients who are on a first-name basis with me now prefer to be on WhatsApp, they don't want to be called. So if there is anything regarding a booking, a pickup, a cancellation, I deal with them on WhatsApp. So during office hours I use the mobile sometimes to communicate with my clients. But otherwise it is restricted, we have emails and we have phones.

Here, we see that despite the restrictions that Mohammed has placed on himself not to check his phone during work hours, and a clear HR policy forbidding such usage, he still does check his phone during work hours. When explaining how he does this, he says that he only checks it once every two hours, and only to see if any close clients require work-related support. This shows how the division of media can occur when individuals in particular roles—in this case, individuals who are both clients and friends—connect through a thread within a particular communication app, while Mohammed connects with others at work primarily in-person and by email.

This example also shows how the potential for constant connectivity creates a bind when workers have ambiguous and complex social relationships. On the one hand, Mohammed's role at work requires that he avoid using his mobile at the office. On the other hand, clients with whom he has a personal relationship expect that he will be available during working hours through a mobile-based app. Mohammed's relationships with these clients who are friends is ambiguous, as these ties straddle multiple roles, which muddies expectations surrounding availability and appropriate media while he is at the office.

Practicing media situatedness, Mohammed reflexively finds a solution to this conundrum. The technical configuration of WhatsApp provides him the opportunity to navigate these tensions by allowing for the exchange of short text-based artifacts in the form of messages, which do not require Mohammed's immediate attention. Drawing on this technical configuration, Mohammed exercises a high degree of reflexive regulation and only checks his mobile the very minimum required times to fit the expectations of his client and his company.

Rules forbidding mobile use at work are not uncommon among knowledge workers more broadly. The survey results in Table 7.4 show that 57% of knowledge workers report that there are rules limiting their mobile use at work. Nevertheless, like Mohammed, 71% of knowledge workers still use their personal phones for work, which implies that they may be using these devices strategically within office environments, and perhaps also outside of office hours.

Mohammed's story is illuminating, as it shows how, even in a regulated office environment where mobiles are forbidden, reflexive mobile use can still occur. It further shows concretely how complex technological configurations on mobile devices—such as the ability to customize ringtones and use specialized messaging apps—allows for a nuanced and reflexive means to navigate these social configurations at work, with family, and with close friends. Yet this technological complexity can also create tensions, because by providing the possibility of constant connection in many forms, it also opens up the potential for new social practices that are potentially at odds with existing social configurations.

Common to other knowledge workers interviewed for this study, Mohammed's ability to manage his communication expectations and resolve tensions around this mobile use stemmed from his relatively high-level position in his company. If he was in a low-paid service or goods producing occupation, he might have lacked the autonomy necessary to ignore the HR policy forbidding mobile use at his office.

Another indicator of media situatedness at work is the intensity and regularity with which individuals communicate with their coworkers through various media. These types of behaviors are difficult to capture in much detail through regular self-report surveys and interviews

Table 7.4. MOBILE USE AT WORK AND LOGGED INTERACTIONS WITH SELECTED WORK TIE

	Knowledge occupation		Service occupation		Public sector occupation		Goods producing occupation	
Use personal phone for work (%)		71		68		37		85
Rules limiting mobile use at work (%)		57		61		86		81
No logged events on personal phone with work tie (%)	Calling	29	Calling	29	Calling	33	Calling	54
	Texting	9	Texting	25	Texting	14	Texting	16
Average events per 10 days with work tie, excluding zero values	Calling	1.3	Calling	1.5	Calling	4.3	Calling	4.4
	Texting	3.6	Texting	4.5	Texting	12.5	Texting	8
Ranking of work tie based on number of logged events (comparison to other ties)	Calling	10	Calling	8	Calling	10	Calling	9
	Texting	10	Texting	8	Texting	10	Texting	9

because respondents often do not accurately recall past interactions in much detail (Boase and Ling 2013; Kobayashi and Boase 2012). As discussed in Chapter 5, as a way of better capturing interaction, this study is unique in that certain nonidentifying mobile calling and texting data were collected from those who completed the app-based version of the survey. Using nonidentifying codes, I was able to identify the time and dates of calls and texts with work ties identified by participants. During the app-based survey, respondents were asked to think of someone they work with and then select that person in their address books or call logs. The app then used a nonidentifying code to identify which calls and texts in the respondent's log history occurred with this particular work tie. Using this approach, I examined patterns of calling and texting with this particular work tie, without collecting their name, phone numbers, or other identifying information.

The results of the logged calling and texting analysis showed that knowledge workers generally used their personal mobiles to text work ties. Seventy-five percent of knowledge workers had at least one logged call with the selected work tie, and 91% had at least one logged text with this same tie. Texting and calling were not very frequent, with knowledge workers averaging 1.3 calls and 3.6 text messages over a 10-day period. In short, these results indicate that personal mobiles may be a useful tool for occasional communication with work ties, but they are not heavily used. Moreover, given that texting is more common than calling, it is likely that the artifact-based nature of texting is helpful in maintaining temporal boundaries.

SERVICE OCCUPATIONS

The interviews with service workers show that although their jobs are often restrictive and low paying, they still manage to develop social practices that help them connect with others inside and outside of work. Throughout these interviews I noticed that service workers that engage with the public often rely on their own personal mobiles as a means of accomplishing various tasks at work.

Gary, a personal trainer, explained that he uses his mobile to phone a fellow staff member at his gym for time sensitive "semi-emergencies," such as when a client is waiting for them. In contrast, with less time-sensitive matters such as coordinating shifts, he draws on texting for one-to-one messages or uses group message chats using Facebook Messenger and SnapChat when coordinating shifts with more than one coworker. Gary's media practices of drawing on synchronous calling for time-sensitive issues and using texting and group message threads for coordination is a common theme among other low-wage workers interviewed in this study.

Gary's reference to coordination of shift work with his colleague is in line with findings from the national survey. Compared to other occupations, workers in service occupations have somewhat less regularity in their working schedules than those working in other occupations. Nearly a third of service workers do not work regular days of the week, possibly because shift work is common in the service industry. Shift work may also explain why a relatively low percentage of these workers (19%) work outside of regular hours.

As found with other service workers, Gary's case illustrates how the provision of services often requires some level of media situatedness when communicating with coworkers. It further shows that these workers respect the temporal boundaries of their coworkers by only using ephemeral communication when interrupting their activities is necessary. Media situatedness requires that Gary reflexively choose a communication medium that will maintain or interrupt the temporal boundaries of his coworker depending on the particular nature of the situation at work. Finally, the very fact that Gary's coworker is reachable through his mobile device makes evident the presence of constant connectivity. Without this availability, Gary's ability to practice media situatedness would be far more limited.

The survey results regarding media use (Table 7.4) show that in contrast to knowledge workers, service workers less commonly exchange detailed informational artifacts by way of email and seem to rely more on artifacts that take the form of short text-based messages. This implies that these workers may be more likely to find themselves in situations where ephemeral communication (in this case, calling) is not appropriate, and the exchange of rich information is not necessary.

While Gary's example shows how service workers use their own devices to coordinate activities with coworkers, the interviews also show several examples of service workers using their own devices to connect with clients and customers. Jing, a piano teacher in her fifties, uses her mobile to schedule lessons with her clients. Although she primarily uses her phone to call and text her friends and family, she uses social media messaging apps (WeChat and Facebook messenger) to connect with her students. Additionally, she uses email to connect with and send documents to the company that recruits and connects her to new clients. Jing admits that she prefers simply to call or text, but with students she uses social media messaging apps because that is what they prefer.

Jing's case shows an example of how the division of media emerges naturally. Although she does not intentionally separate her clients into social media messaging apps and her other relationships into calling and texting, this occurs because she recognizes the preferences of her students. This reflexive recognition is also an example of media situatedness in that it shows how individuals choose media based on a variety of factors, some of which may be unique particular relationships. Finally, the use of messaging apps rather than ephemeral media shows how temporal boundaries are maintained through the use of artifact-based media.

In other cases, service workers found that being constantly available in the context of work created undesirable situations. Several respondents mentioned situations in which they were part of group messaging threads with workmates, despite feeling that they would rather not be involved in these interactions. For example, Will, a car salesperson in his thirties, is part of a WhatsApp group message thread in which salespeople share information at his dealership. This small group of salespeople has several threads that they use to share information about customers, and outside of work they use other threads to arrange social get-togethers. At times, Will feels uncomfortable constantly communicating in this type of forum. Nevertheless, he feels obligated to take part in these group threads.

I think it's the sense that I want to know what's going on. I want to stay informed. With work I have to be. I have to do that because I need to know what cars are sold and what is still available, and that information is available in the group chat, unfortunately. Um or else, if I didn't need it, I would just not have WhatsApp because I don't like group chats.

PUBLIC SECTOR OCCUPATIONS

As with knowledge workers, participants working in public sector occupations practiced media situatedness as a means of meeting their social obligations. However, workers in these public sector occupations often had somewhat more restrictive social roles than knowledge workers. This is not surprising, given that these roles tend to exist in large organizations such as hospitals and schools, where there are long-standing traditions, rules, and professional practices.

Susan, an elementary teacher in her fifties, explained her temporal boundaries at work as they apply when a family member attempts to get in touch with her:

> If it's an emergency my family will call the school, however, otherwise they'll text me. But they're also very aware that I may not get to them that day. Like, normally I will, because I'll check my phone maybe two or three times a day. But if it's something really important [they will call], like when my husband called the school and had the secretary literally buzz my classroom and tell me, "Your husband is picking up at 3:30". Great, thank you very much.

This quote reveals several themes. First, Susan's role as a teacher prevents her from receiving calls on her mobile during the day and limits the time that she has to check for new text messages. When a family member needs to get in touch with her for an emergency or other time-sensitive matter, they must communicate using the social rules developed around older communication media at her school. These rules require that the communication occur not only through a phone but also through another worker within the organization and a PA system that can be heard by students in her classroom. These social restrictions create a temporal boundary that can only be breached on rare occasions, and only for reasons that would be considered appropriate in her organization.

At the same time, the fact that Susan checks her mobile two or three times a day shows that these temporal boundaries can be breached in certain ways. Her mobile creates the potential for direct communication while she is at school by receiving artifact-based texts and allowing her to receive them visually in a way that will not draw attention to her or interrupt the flow of activities. Here, we see that even in a fairly restrictive environment, the potential for connection created by mobiles allows Susan to practice some degree of media situatedness. It is also an example of the divisions of media because non-time-sensitive interactions occur through the medium of mobile texts, while other interactions are in-person or over the PA system in her classroom.

Susan's story is not unique. Workers in public sector organizations must contend with media practices that have been formed over decades, often in organizations that have a majority of their workers colocated in large buildings. This means that communication has been optimized for in-person interactions. The development of constant connectivity and technological complexity has created a situation in which workers are now more available for mobile interactions. At the same time, the legacy of in-person interaction in their working environments still places heavy restrictions on mobile communication. It is through mediated situatedness that workers in these institutions exercise some level of communicative autonomy, if only in short bursts throughout the day.

GOODS PRODUCING OCCUPATIONS

Interviews with workers in goods production generally show that these workers have the most constraints on their communication practices at work. In some cases, these constraints were so great that these workers

At Work   149

simply did not have the opportunity to develop mediated communication practices. Ryan, who works at a chemical plant, is a prime example of how these restrictions leave little opportunity for mediated communication. When asked if his job provides him with any autonomy to make any important decisions at work, he responded, "Our job is very procedural . . . . Almost any decision deviating from procedure we have to discuss with our superior. So the answer to that is never." Ryan works eight-hour shifts, during which he has little opportunity to interact with others. Describing his typical day, he explained,

> The supervisor will assign you what to do, and you are pretty on your own for the rest of the shift. Unless of course you are deviating from procedure, you need help to do something. Then you ask somebody for help, or tell the supervisor the situation and you need to do something.

Rules about mobile phone use while on the job are equally clear: "They don't like anyone using cellphones on the compound—not on the compound, not in the building." For this reason, all of Ryan's mobile use occurs outside of work hours. Ryan's situation at work shows how temporal boundaries exist as part of larger social configurations at work and how he lacks the power to breach these boundaries, even by digital means.

While Ryan's story is instructive and speaks to the lack of power that was common among good producing workers in the survey, construction workers had somewhat more autonomy to use their devices on the job. For example, Dennis works part-time in construction, and he found his job through his close friend who manages construction projects. Dennis knows that when he wants to connect with his friend during work hours, it is best to call him directly on his work phone:

> Ah, well I'll typically ring him on his work phone when he's at work, if he needs me. Outside of work it's mainly Messenger. Occasionally it's WhatsApp. Again I think it's whatever it's convenient for either of us at the time, sort of thing.

Dennis' explanation shows a level of media situatedness in that he knows the most appropriate means of connecting with his friend in the context of work-related communication. The choice of using an ephemeral medium for work-related communication and artifact-based media for non-working matters further implies that temporal boundaries can be breached in this occupation. Dennis's case also shows a blurring of work and friendship, which complicates his relationship and increases the need for media situatedness.

In sum, the interviews conducted for this study show how rigid and constraining roles in goods producing occupations can severely limit the opportunity that individuals have to exercise reflexive communication practices. While public sector workers also occupied rigid social roles at work, they generally had more opportunity to exert some level of control over their communication in particular circumstances. Furthermore, while there were some examples of goods producing workers exercising some amount of autonomy over their communication, these examples were not very common. These interview results help to explain why the results of the national survey show that compared to workers in other occupations, the range of media used by goods producing workers is generally quite low and is most commonly limited to in-person communication. These results are also consistent with the theories of social complexity discussed in Chapter 3.

CONCLUSION

In this chapter, I explored the social implications of constant connectivity in the context of work. In order to approach this topic, I examined how practices of connection vary between different types of occupations. The review of sociological literature provided in Chapter 3 indicates that occupation directly influences personal network complexity. This literature shows that knowledge and service workers are often required to actively manage complex professional networks. Given that personal network complexity is a type of social configuration that can be maintained and perpetuated by practices of connection, it is reasonable to expect that these practices will differ somewhat between different occupations. Understanding how practices of connection vary between occupations provides further insight into the social implications of constant connectivity.

Overall, I find support for the theory that the knowledge and service occupations that dominate many contemporary economies entail different kinds of institutional, relational, and temporal complexity. Knowledge and service workers must contend with relational and role ambiguity and actively manage interactions with others while at work. As a means of dealing with these social configurations, they draw on a variety of media (between and within communication apps), and they configure their media in ways that are consistent with their situations. In this way, technological complexity is congruent with social complexity.

As knowledge and service workers draw on various media to connect with others in the context of work, they practice media situatedness by reflexively considering their current situations and choosing media that best suit these situations. A division of media emerges as they sometimes accommodate the media preferences of others—such as when Mohammed checks WhatsApp for messages from his close clients and email from his other clients, or when Jing uses social media apps to communicate with her students and email to communicate with her office. Knowledge and service workers also draw on media in ways that help them to maintain the temporal boundaries at work.

In contrast to knowledge and service workers, I find that those working in the public sector and goods producing occupations generally face stronger restrictions at work, which are part of the more rigid social roles they occupy. In the case of public sector workers, tensions can arise when their roles at work are in conflict with their relational roles with family and friends. This is most evident when family or friends outside of work attempt to communicate with them while they are on the job. In these cases, social configurations at work create temporal boundaries, which can be difficult for those outside of work to breach. However, I generally find that public sector workers have ways of resolving these tensions, such as when Susan finds time to check her phone for messages during brief periods throughout the day. Ultimately, while these public sector employees occupy roles that assume stringent temporal boundaries, they still have some level of power in the face of competing obligations. This finding is in line with Coser's theory of role complexity discussed in Chapter 3, as it shows that certain large institutions and practices endure even in a knowledge- and service-focused economy.

Workers in goods producing occupations have the most restrictive working environment. These workers often occupy highly prescriptive roles that afford them little time or autonomy to communicate with others outside of work. Even at work, their communication with coworkers and managers appears to be fairly minimal and limited to in-person interactions. Accordingly, their mediated communication practices are quite limited, as these workers are not given the power to exercise media situatedness, communicate with different relationships over multiple channels, or break the temporal boundaries placed on them at work. Again, we see that Coser's theory linking occupational status with autonomy and social complexity still applies to low-wage goods producing workers. Although Coser does not consider the impact that restrictive roles play on practices of connection, the finding that these workers lack the autonomy to exercise media situatedness or engage others by technological means is consistent with her theoretical framework.

While this study has focused on workers living in Canada, to the extent that these different types of occupations exist in other countries, it is reasonable to expect similar practices of connection to emerge. To the extent that knowledge, service, public sector, and goods producing occupations entail similar expectations from workers, we can expect that workers within those occupations will have similar communication practices. However, to fully test this conjecture, further research is necessary.

In sum, although the three common practices of connection exist to some extent in all occupations, workers have the most control over these practices in knowledge-based occupations and the least control in goods producing occupations. Taken together, these results show how the social implications of constant connectivity are shaped by power in the context of work.

8

With Family

In this chapter, I will draw on the results of the study to explore the social implications of constant connectivity in the context of family. Specifically, I will discuss how media situatedness, the division of media, and temporal boundaries stem from and perpetuate social and technological complexity in the context of family life.

As discussed in Chapter 3, contemporary family relationships are complexly configured. The decline of the nuclear family has coincided with a rise in new family arrangements, such as cohabitation, same-sex unions, childless partnerships, or simply people living alone and maintaining family relationships at a distance. Divorce is not uncommon, and individuals may move between partnerships in which they have multiple children, stepchildren, and custody arrangements. At the same time, the percentage of adults choosing not to have children has increased. All of this implies that relationships with family members must now be actively constructed and maintained. Rather than following rigid and enduring social roles, individuals often reflexively decide how and when to interact with family members. These interactions are further complicated by the temporal complexity that arises when family members outside and within the household have different work schedules and social commitments.

In order to understand the practices of connection that emerge within the complex social context of family life, I focus on the practices of connection that occur within four types of family relationships: partners

The Digital Bind. Jeffrey Boase, Oxford University Press. © Oxford University Press (2025).
DOI: 10.1093/oso/9780197798591.003.0009

and spouses, parents and children, supportive family relationships, and diverse family relationships. Before exploring these relationships, I will briefly provide some contextual information regarding common household arrangements in Canada.

FAMILY ARRANGEMENTS IN CANADA

The sociological literature indicates that family arrangements have become more complex over time, and this complexity is reflected in the Canadian national surveys used in this study (see Table 8.1). A third of the adult participants live with only a partner or spouse, and nearly another third live with a partner or spouse and children.[1] Although these two arrangements are most common, arrangements in the remaining households were diverse. Sixteen percent of these adult respondents live with at least one parent, 12% live alone, 9% live with someone else, and 5% are single parents. The diversity of family arrangements in Canada was further reflected in the variety of family members discussed during the in-depth interviews. Having established that the complexity of family life is captured in this study, I will now provide an in-depth analysis of how practices of connection stem from and perpetuate this complexity by discussing four types of family relationships.

Table 8.1. HOUSEHOLD COMPOSITION OF RESPONDENTS

Living situation	%
Lives alone	12
Lives with partner/spouse only	33
Lives with child(ren) only	5
Lives with child(ren) and partner/spouse	30
Adult living with parent(s)	16
Lives with someone else	9

PARTNERS AND SPOUSES

I will begin this section by reviewing results from the national surveys in order to determine general patterns of media use with partners and spouses. I will then draw on the in-depth interviews to show how these general patterns are indicative of media situatedness and temporal boundaries.

Survey results show that respondents tend to use more media on a weekly basis with their spouses and partners than with other family members (see Table 8.2). Moreover, compared to interactions with other family members, interactions with partners and spouses more often included several types of artifact-based media: texting, email, and social media messaging. In contrast, interactions with other family members more commonly relied only on texting or on social media messaging, which is functionally quite similar to texting. The use of email within any kind of family relationships may not seem intuitive, as email use is often associated with professional relationships. However, when considering that email allows for the exchange of detailed information such as household bills, its use between couples living in the same home makes sense.

The self-reported survey results presented in Table 8.2 do not provide any information about the frequency or regularity of media use. In order to have a better understanding of frequency and regularity with ephemeral calling and artifact-based texting, I draw on the results of my analysis focused on logged calls and texts with these various family ties (see Table 8.3).

In general, these results show that there is more frequent calling and texting with spouses and partners than with other family ties. However, these results also suggest that calling and texting is not something that individuals constantly engage in many times per day. For example, even among spouses and partners, there is an average of 5.1 logged calls and 22.6 logged texts per 10 days. In other words, individuals tend to call their partners an average of once every other day and exchange about two text messages per day.

Table 8.2. REPORTED MEDIATED INTERACTIONS WITH SELECTED FAMILY TIE IN THE PAST WEEK

	Family at home					Family outside home			
	Spouse/partner		Child		Parent		Supportive tie that provides important help		Diverse tie that holds different political views	
Average number of media used	3.5		3		3.1		2.7		1.8	
5 most used media, excluding in-person communication (%)	Called	79	Texted	69	Called	80	Called	72	In-person	52
	Texted	70	Called	48	Texted	76	In-person	57	Called	40
	Emailed	37	Social media messaged	29	Social media messaged	19	Texted	55	Texted	32
	Social media messaged	29	Read post(s)	26	Read post(s)	17	Emailed	27	Social media messaged	20
	Read post(s)	28	Emailed	16	Emailed	2	Social media messaged	25	Emailed	14

3 most common media combinations, including in-person communication (%)	Emailed, texted, called and in-person	15	Texted, called and in-person	20	Texted, called and in-person	33	Texted, called and in-person	20	Called only	11
	Texted, called and in-person	15	Texted and in-person	14	Emailed, texted, called and in-person	10	Called only	7	Texted and in-person	11
	Social media messaged, texted, called and in-person	12	In-person only	7	Texted and in-person	10	Called and in-person	7	In-person only	10

In order to better understand the regularity of calling and texting with spouses and partners, I conducted a dispersion analysis. In this analysis, all individuals with whom there is logged calling are ranked according to how evenly calls and texts are dispersed on a weekly basis throughout their entire logged history. For example, if respondent A calls their spouse at least once a week more regularly than they call any other person in their call log, then their spouse would be ranked first and have a score of 1. In this way, the rankings provided in this analysis are relative to other social ties with whom respondents have called or texted.

The results presented in Table 8.3 indicate that respondents have more regular calling with spouses and partners than with other family ties. In other words, on a weekly basis, individuals more consistently call their spouses and partners than they call and text other family ties. These results also show that they have a relatively higher regularity of texting with their spouses and partners than with most other ties.

In sum, these patterns of media use at the population level indicate that compared to other family ties, respondents draw on a wider range of media to connect with their spouses and partners. They also have generally more frequent and regular calling and texting with their spouses and partners than other family ties.

The in-depth interviews provide insight into the practices of connection underlying these general population–level statistics. They show that respondents draw on many media to communicate with their spouses and partners, and do so frequently and regularly, as a means of practicing media situatedness and maintaining temporal boundaries. I will now turn to one particular interview because it helps to explain these general trends and because it tells a story that is similar to the stories told by other participants.

Jason, a native of Hong Kong who works as an assistant manager in Vancouver, connects with his spouse through a variety of media, including calling, texting, and several social media messaging apps. With each of these apps, he considers the content of the exchange as well as the urgency of the situation.

Table 8.3. Logged interactions with selected family tie

		Family at home			Family outside home	
		Spouse/partner	Child	Parent	Supportive tie that provides important help	Diverse tie that holds different political views
Calls	Zero logged calls with tie (%)	2	9	2	11	16
	Average calls per 10 days with tie, excluding zero values	5.1	3.7	3.8	2.6	2.3
	Ranking of tie based on number of logged calls[*]	2	2	3	4	6
	Ranking of tie based on weekly dispersion of logged calls[*]	2	5	3	4	7
Texts	Zero logged texts with tie (%)	22	19	19	26	25
	Average texts per 10 days with tie, excluding zero values	22.6	17.7	11.1	17	11.7
	Ranking of tie based on number of logged texts[*]	1	2	3	4	7
	Ranking of tie based on weekly dispersion of logged texts[*]	4	3	3	6	9

[*] Lower scores indicate a higher ranking. Scores are the median values of tie ranking across all respondents.

> WhatsApp is more like easy going things. It's not important, but like [texting] or calling your wife . . . is more important. Or like, more urgent that you need [an] immediate response . . . let's say if I'm picking her up, right, and like she's not replying on WhatsApp, then [I] may wanna text her, to make sure that she got my message, right. Um, or like if she's not even replying, then I may just call her to check if things are okay.

Here, we can see that Jason's general approach with urgent matters is to first use WhatApp, which he considers to be most casual. If that does not lead to a response, he then uses regular texting as a means of conveying greater urgency. Failing a response by texting, he will break a temporal boundary and call her directly. Although messages sent by WhatsApp and the default texting app function in similar ways, Jason is using them to convey different meanings. The fact that he associates WhatsApp with "easygoing things" further implies that this meaning is shared with his spouse, and his use of this medium over texting is intended to imply something to his spouse about the nature of the situation.

Although the selection of medium implies something about the nature of the situation, later Jason clarifies that it can also relate to the content of the message itself.

> Sometimes texting her, like, she can reply later on too right. Like WhatsApp text or SMS text. And it doesn't have to be like an immediate response right . . . they can think about it and then [provide] feedback later on, um . . . . Yeah, and then sometimes you may just want to let her know something.

Like 37% of the respondents in the national surveys, Jason exchanges email with his spouse. He does this three or four times a week "because we forward or share all the bills, right. So, those things, function wise, that you have to reply with an email with an attachment, then you use the email."

Jason's mediated communication practices with his spouse show how media situatedness arises as cohabitating partners and spouses communicate with each other in a variety of contexts throughout the day. In some contexts, the urgency of the communication factors most heavily into the medium that Jason selects. This approach to media selection further shows how he attempts to maintain temporal boundaries with his partner and breaks them through ephemeral voice calling only when he feels the urgency of the situation requires him to do so. In other contexts, Jason considers the content of the message to be most critical when selecting a medium. If he feels his spouse may need some time to think about something he wants to share with her, he will send short message artifacts through WhatsApp or the default texting app. If the content of a message is to do with financially related coordination, he will use email, as it easily allows for the attachment of financial documents.

Jason's approach to communicating with his spouse was shared by many of the other respondents interviewed for this study. By practicing media situatedness, they are able to maintain temporal boundaries throughout the day while still coordinating activities and sharing information.

CHILDREN AND PARENTS

The results of the national surveys show that respondents often draw on several media when communicating with parents and children living in the same household (see Table 8.2). When communicating with their children in the past week, 69% of the respondents reported texting, while 48% reported calling, and 29% reported using social media messaging. In contrast, when communicating with parents in the past week, 80% reported calling, 76% reported texting, and 19% reported social media messaging.[2] With both parents and children, the combinations of media most commonly used in the previous week were texting, calling, and in-person interaction.

The results of the logged calling and texting analysis provided in Table 8.3 show relatively frequent and regular calling and texting with children and parents living in the same home. These results are generally similar but somewhat lower than the frequency and regularity of calls and texts with spouses and partners.

The in-depth interviews show the practices of connection underlying the population-level results. In several of the interviews, participants discussed the practice of media situatedness when they explained that their choice of medium was often based on knowledge of what their parent or child was doing at a particular time and their media preferences. Valeria, a software engineer in her twenties who lives with her parents explains an example of how media situatedness occurs when contacting her mother.

> I message her a lot. I Facebook Message my mom because she doesn't check her phone during the day. But at work she'll check her Messenger, because she always has her Facebook open. So I know that from 9 to 5, if I need my mom, it's easy to—it's easier to send her a message through my laptop, on Messenger than to like, grab my phone and call her 'cuz she won't . . . probably reply.

In addition to showing media situatedness, this example also shows how Valeria's knowledge of her mother's work schedule and media preferences allows her to select a medium that will pass through the temporal boundary that her mother creates by not using her phone at work.

The division of media is quite apparent in mediated communication practices that occur with nonadult children. This is because children often want to keep their interactions with their parents separate from their peer interactions. For example, Anika explains how her teenage son only responds to text messages, even in urgent situations. "In an emergency I have to text him because he doesn't answer his phone. [laughs] First I'd text him then I don't hear—I don't get back his message. Then I call him. And again I text him." When asked if she is connected to her son through social media, she explained that she was connected to him through Facebook, but "I don't see though his posts now. Maybe he disfriended me. [laughs] I haven't seen anything from him in a long time." Anika's relationship with her son also shows that although the possibility of constant connectivity can be potentially used by parents to exercise control over their children's lives, this control is not always effective.

With Family

Although her son appears to be purposefully maintaining temporal and social boundaries with Anika, it is also clear that their mediated connections are still an important part of their relationship. Anika explains that her son is part of her family group texting threads on WhatsApp, which include several family members living in India. "On WhatsApp... it's a fun thing, on a group message, there is something going on, you know sibling and family. It's a fun thing. Fun talk is sometimes going on. And some comments we don't want to put in a group but we both [laughs] send to them each other." Anika's back-channeling with her son through one-on-one comment threads about family group messages shows that despite the fact her son maintains a division of media, they still connect positively through certain apps.

The interviews show that communication between parents and children not living in the same home was generally regular, but less frequent, and more often limited to just one medium. Respondents with older parents tended to use mainly landline phones because this is what their parents preferred. In Susan's words, "Well, actually we, the only reason why we still have it is for my mother and my father-in-law who are in their 80s and there's no way they'd be able to learn a new phone number."

While most respondents indicated that connecting with their geographically distant parents was an important part of their lives, at times these interactions are not always viewed as optimal. Natalie, a participant in her fifties, explained,

> The only time that I don't want to use the phone is when I call my mom. My mom likes to talk a lot. I can be on the phone for two hours with her and it's like, ugh. But I have to call her so then I put the phone I put my earbuds on, put the phone in my pocket and I walk around the house and take care of my business while listening to her.

Natalie's calls with her mother are a prime example of how the potential for constant connectivity can put us in a bind. Nevertheless, although her availability by way of mobile media results in interactions that she finds less than ideal, the portability of connecting to her mobile with earbuds still allows her some level of autonomy.

In sum, the results of the population-level survey and the in-depth interviews all show that respondents engage in media situatedness, the division of media, and temporal boundaries within child and parent relationships. It should be noted that unlike the partner and spousal relationships explored in the previous section, the role of power was more apparent in the communication practices between parents and their adolescent children. The desire that adolescents have to maintain temporal boundaries through the use of asynchronous media can create tension with their parents who would prefer to know more about their social lives and activities.

SUPPORTIVE FAMILY MEMBERS LIVING OUTSIDE OF THE HOME

As discussed in Chapter 3, many contemporary family relationships require active and voluntary maintenance. This is particularly true for relationships with family members living outside of the home, as they do not require daily copresence. In this section, I explore the practices of connection that occur with supportive family members living outside of the home. Compared to household family members, these relationships require more active maintenance, and considering that they are supportive further implies that there is the motivation to stay connected with these members.

Overall, the results of the population-level surveys show that the patterns of media use with supportive family members living outside of the home are not drastically different from the patterns of media use with household members. As shown in Table 8.2, respondents drew on a variety of media in the previous week to maintain contact with these supportive family members. Moreover, even though they lived outside of the home, 57% of the respondents reported meeting with these supportive family ties in the previous week. Calling and texting were also common methods of staying connected to these relationships.

The results regarding the frequency and regularity of calling and texting with supportive family ties who live outside of the home are shown in Table 8.3. Overall, these results show slightly less frequent and regular calling and texting with these ties compared to household members. Nevertheless, compared to the many other individuals that respondents called and texted, these values are still relatively high.

Overall, the population-level results supported the literature reviewed in Chapter 3 by showing that individuals actively maintain contact with these nonhousehold supportive family relationships.

The in-depth interviews conducted for this project showed more clearly the motivations for this active connection. They revealed that although these relationships were often deeply valued, communication typically happens either when a need arises or just as a means of staying in touch on a regular basis. These relationships are not necessarily as emotionally close as those with household family, even though they provide valuable support.

Michelle's relationship with her brother typifies this dynamic. In Michelle's words, "We're not very close but at the same time I know if I need something then he's there to help or he needs something, I'm there." Michelle will typically text him when

> I need his help then I text him more or we need to talk about any family stuff we text each other . . . . We talk on the phone or occasionally, to catch up. Socialize occasionally, but it's mostly about something practical . . . even in person, what we talk about is very to the point. He doesn't like socializing too much, so we don't talk about other things like my work related or his work related things.

Michelle's relationship with her brother shows a degree of active maintenance and a desire to connect for "practical" reasons as new situations in her life unfold. Media situatedness appears as she draws on calling for "catching up" and texting for family matters in which she needs support. Other respondents felt that the ephemeral nature of calling more easily allowed for maintaining a sense of connection, while texting was most appropriate when unexpected issues arose and they wanted to maintain temporal boundaries.

Other supportive family relationships discussed during the interviews showed similar approaches to media situatedness, even when there were greater levels of emotional connection and frequent contact. These types of supportive relationships were most often with parents who live further away. For example, Conor's mom lives about two and a half hours away. He exchanges texts with her for a variety of reasons:

> We text about plans typically. Changing stuff, like if a family member is like in an accident something like that. Um and if we need to meet for Christmas or something, and that's about . . . . Also I guess about updates in my life. And regular communication stuff is about once a week to catch up. And the rest of it, obviously a few times a year . . . . I typically use calling for support or getting a lot of information. You know like having multiple plans, like kind of something that back more ideas for me. Like considering A, B and C, here are pros and cons, what do you think?

Conor's use of texting to coordinate, update, and maintain regular contact with his mother shows that he generally reserves this medium for communication that does not require much deliberation. In contrast, when he needs support with a difficult decision, he uses calling. This approach to media situatedness is an example of how respondents actively draw on media in a variety of situations as a means of receiving support and staying connected to their supportive family members.

In sum, the results of my study show that individuals draw on a variety of media to maintain supportive connections with family ties living outside of their household. This requires a high degree of media situatedness. It is notable that respondents in the in-depth interviews did not often mention that they intentionally seek a division of media or try to maintain temporal boundaries. However, their common use of artifact-based texting to exchange useful information suggests that they would prefer not to interrupt the activities of these family members or face these interruptions themselves. Moreover, it is likely that these supportive members are not directly connected to their friends and colleagues, so the division of media emerges naturally with these relationships.

POLITICALLY DIVERSE FAMILY MEMBERS LIVING OUTSIDE OF THE HOME

In order to diversify the set of family members studied in this project, I asked respondents to report on their interactions with family members living outside of their homes who hold political views that are significantly different from their own. Given that contemporary family relationships tend to require active maintenance, it is reasonable to expect that patterns of media use would be unique for these ties. This is because there may be less desire to interact with these ties given that interaction has the potential to lead to interpersonal tension and conflict.

The population-level survey results indeed show less diverse media use with these family ties. As shown in Table 8.2, unlike the other family relationships examined in this study, respondents rarely drew on multiple media in the previous week to connect with politically diverse family ties. As indicated in Table 8.3, this is likely because they have less frequent and regular communication with these ties compared to other family ties. It could be inferred from these results that when there is little desire to connect with these ties, respondents simply do not make the effort to stay in active communication with them.

The in-depth interviews showed that more than with other family ties, participants tended to be strategic in their communication with politically diverse family ties. Caitlin's relationship with her mother shows how this can occur. Although Caitlin feels very close to her mother, she knows that their differing views can be a source of tension. "If I'm being completely honest, if I don't wanna talk to her on the phone and I feel like I haven't connected in a while, I'll just text instead of picking up the phone and calling." Caitlin lives in the same city as her mother, and she will visit occasionally. During these visits she will mostly discuss "what she's been up to, what I've been doing, same sort of things [as texting]. I avoid politics and religion."

Caitlin's decision to text rather than call allows her to strategically avoid politics and religion by keeping her messages on topic. Unlike other examples where media situatedness occurs based on situations as they arise, Caitlin's preference for texting her mother shows how this situatedness can also be influenced by broader relational dynamics.

In sum, the results support the thesis that connecting with family reflects the individualistic nature of contemporary family life. Relationships must be actively maintained by the individual, and if there is no desire to do so, they often exist in a state of dormancy. When respondents feel that they need to connect with politically diverse family members, they practice media situatedness by drawing primarily on artifact-based media that help them to avoid unpleasant interactions.

CONCLUSION

The results of this study show how individuals actively manage complex family networks by drawing on the many communication options available to them. In doing so, they enact the three common practices of connection discussed in Chapter 6 as a means of navigating this social complexity. However, the context in which the practices of connection are enacted is quite different from the occupational contexts discussed in the previous chapter. With family relationships, particular types of relationships often entail unique considerations as individuals reflexively draw on communication media in their practices of connection. I conclude this chapter by discussing how these findings reflect the many roles that individuals play within families as they connect with complexly configured family networks.

The factors that influence media choices as respondents practice media situatedness vary considerably between different types of family ties. When communicating with spouses, partners, children, and parents living in the same household, media situatedness occurs as individuals coordinate activities and stay in touch throughout the day. In contrast, when interacting with nonhousehold supportive family members, respondents practice media situatedness by considering the nature of the support that they wish to receive and choose a medium that is most suitable for the reception of that support. When interacting with nonhousehold politically diverse family members, media situatedness occurs as respondents reflexively chose artifact-based media that help them to avoid tension and conflict.

The factors that influence the division of media also vary between different types of family ties. Teens attempt to use media channels with their parents that are different from those that they use with their peers. This creates tensions, indicating the imbalance of power within parent and child relationships. In contrast, the division of media occurs more naturally with other kinds of family relationships. This is likely because power is less influential in media selection with these relationships, and as a result, the division of media occurs as different apps are selected for use with different family members based on a variety of situational factors.

In the case of temporal boundaries, respondents draw on artifact-based media to avoid interrupting their household members as they coordinate activities through the day. With supportive family ties living outside of the home, temporal boundaries are less of a consideration, as it is the type of support desired that largely influences media selection. In the case of politically diverse relationships with family members living outside of the home, temporal boundaries are more the by-product of choosing artifact-based media as a means of avoiding conflict.

In sum, the social implications of constant connectivity in the context of family are varied. This is because the complexity of family relationships often requires that individuals reflexively draw on the complex media options available to them. It is through the combination of constant connectivity and technological complexity that individuals have the technological means necessary to fully practice media situatedness and the division of media, and to maintain temporal boundaries. These practices, in turn, help individuals maintain and perpetuate social complexity in the context of family life, thereby deepening the embedding of technology into family life.

9

With Friends

Having discussed the social implications of constant connectivity in the context of work and family, I will now turn to the context of friendship. As in the previous two chapters, I will consider how practices of connection stem from and perpetuate relational complexity.

While it is clear that work and family relationships have become more complex, they are still grounded to some extent in institutional roles. By comparison, friendships most exemplify personal network complexity in that friendship roles are more actively constructed and maintained. In Chapter 3, I discussed several dimensions of social ties, including emotional closeness, supportiveness, intimacy (mutual exchanges), and duration. Although close relationships are traditionally assumed to be high on all of these dimensions, my discussion of personal network complexity suggests that this may not be the case with contemporary friendships. For example, some friendships may be relatively recent yet include high levels of emotional closeness and intimate exchange. Other friendships may endure over long periods of time and involve only infrequent supportive exchanges.

Instead of conflating several dimensions of friendship, in this chapter, I will separately consider friendship ties that are close, enduring, supportive, and that are politically diverse. This will allow us to understand the nuanced differences between these various dimensions of friendship and how they relate to practices of connection in the presence of constant connectivity.

The Digital Bind. Jeffrey Boase, Oxford University Press. © Oxford University Press (2025).
DOI: 10.1093/oso/9780197798591.003.0010

CLOSE FRIENDSHIPS

Emotional closeness is a trait that people often use to distinguish their very close friends from other friends. Marsden and Campbell (1984) find this type of closeness to be the best overall indicator of tie strength, although, as I argue in Chapter 3, this concept itself oversimplifies the relational complexity that exists in contemporary relationships. Nevertheless, by examining just one important dimension of friendship, we are able to understand the extent to which practices of connection relate to this dimension.

In the survey and interviews, participants were asked to think first about one friend to whom they "feel very close" and then another friend to whom they feel "somewhat close." Participants reported the various ways that they had connected with each of these friends during the previous week and how they knew them. The survey data gathered from this approach allows us to see common patterns of media use and how they vary by closeness, and the in-depth interviews further help us to understand why these patterns exist. Those respondents that completed the app-based version of the survey further selected their very close and somewhat close friends from their address book, and this generated nonidentifying codes that allowed us to identify the times and dates of calls and texts with these ties.

The survey results show that respondents used similar media with their very close and somewhat close ties in the previous week, but not to the same extent (see Table 9.1). Texting is the most commonly used medium with very close friends (65%) and somewhat close friends (51%), followed by in-person interaction (61% and 44%, respectively), calling (60% and 27%), and social media messaging (40% and 23%). These results also show that participants drew on a greater number of media throughout the week with their very close friends (2.8 on average) than with their somewhat close friends (1.9 on average).

Analysis of the logged calling and texting data generally shows clear differences between very close and somewhat close friends (see Table 9.2). Overall, these results show that respondents call and text their very close friends more frequently and regularly than their somewhat

	Very close friend		Somewhat close friend		Supportive friend (provides important help)		Diverse friend (different political views)	
Average number of media used	2.8		1.9		2.3		1.6	
5 most used media (excluding in-person communication)	Texted	65	Texted	51	Texted	66	Texted	37
	In-person	61	In-person	44	In-person	58	In-person	32
	Called	60	Called	27	Called	46	Social media messaged	27
	Social media messaged	40	Social media messaged	23	Read post(s)	25	Called	26
	Emailed	25	Read post(s)	18	Social media messaged	22	Read post(s)	25
Most common media combinations	Social media messaged, texted, called and in-person	13	Texted only	9	Texted, called and in-person	13	Social media messaged only	11
	Texted, called and in-person	9	Texted and in-person	8	Texted and in-person	8	Called and in-person	8
	Texted only	6	Texted, called and in-person	7	Social media messaged only	6	Texted and in-person	8

close friends. Their average number of calls with their very close friends per ten-day period is more than twice as high as with somewhat close friends (an average of 2.6 versus 1.0). The average number of texts in the same period is approximately 4 times higher for very close friends than somewhat close friends (an average of 23.7 versus 6.5). However, even among very close friends, these results do not show that calling and texting are occurring constantly throughout the day. Rather, they seem to be an important way that individuals connect with their friends, but not to the point where it is consuming a great deal of their attention.

The in-depth interviews generally show that texting is used both for coordination and for keeping a sense of connection within friendships, while calling is more often used to provide emotional support. This is particularly common among younger respondents. Joanna, a student in her twenties, explained how she maintains contact with a very close friend that she has known since childhood.

I usually text about things that happened in my life or like, ask her questions about how she's doing. Um, then sometimes we like to talk about shows that we've been watching. That's the . . . majority just talking about shows we watched [chuckles]. That happens a lot.

In contrast, Joanna unwillingly uses calling with this friend to exchange emotional support, explaining that it is more immediate than texting.

Yeah, uh, calling is . . . I don't enjoy it. But if it's someone I know well, and I know that they'd be able to help me if I did call them, I would do that. Like, usually if one of us is upset, and we're like "I just need someone to talk to." So then we chat over the phone rather than just, you know, waiting for people to respond and taking up, like time doing that.

Joanna's explanation shows how media situatedness can occur in very close friendships. Calling is generally only considered appropriate for

Table 9.2. LOGGED INTERACTIONS WITH SELECTED FRIEND TIE

		Close friend	Somewhat close friend	Supportive friend (provides important help)	Diverse friend (different political views)
Calls	Zero logged calls with tie (%)	17	44	17	36
	Average calls per 10 days with tie, excluding zero values	2.6	1	2	0.9
	Ranking of tie based on number of logged calls*	4	7	6	7
	Ranking of tie based on weekly dispersion of logged calls*	5	10	7	12
Texts	Zero logged texts with tie (%)	22	17	10	16
	Average texts per 10 days with tie, excluding zero values	23.7	6.5	37.6	4.1
	Ranking of tie based on number of logged texts*	5	9	6	12
	Ranking of tie based on weekly dispersion of logged texts*	5	9	7	13

* Lower scores indicate higher rankings. Scores are the median values of tie ranking across all respondents.

the exchange of emotional support, while texting is used for keeping connected and planning activities. Texting also helps respondents maintain temporal boundaries while at the same time maintaining consistent daily contact, regardless of other activities that are happening throughout the day.

Although respondents in their twenties generally avoided voice calls, older respondents called in a diverse range of situations, even though texting is still the primary way they stay connected with their friends. Tricia, a payroll contractor in her sixties, often draws on a combination of calling and texting to connect with her very close and somewhat close friends.

> Something comes up, you know, [my best friend] could text me, and you know whether it's in their opinion whether she's asking me something whether we're gonna meet whether it's you know she's sending me a link to something whether it's you know a recipe and stuff like that, or whether it's you know something that she's bought for her grandchild, or something like that. So I would say like, you know, my best friend, I would be talking to her like, you know, through some kind of communication, you know, every other day. My other girlfriends, I would say, either calling or texting, once a week, for sure.

Consistent with the survey results, Tricia communicates with her very close friend more often than her somewhat close friend but communicates using similar media. Her narrative also shows how emotional closeness may drive the communication frequency. Her mixing of communication media arises through a media situatedness approach that considers temporal boundaries, social norms that vary by age, and the desire for more emotionally intense exchanges.

In sum, these results show that practices of connection have been deeply embedded into close friendships. Within both very close and somewhat close friendships, respondents practiced media situatedness as a means of staying connected to these ties while still respecting temporal boundaries. Moreover, while respondents did not discuss this explicitly, their use of communication media to directly connect with close friendships individually, rather than through friendship groups, implies that they are maintaining a division of media.

ENDURING FRIENDSHIPS

The existence of enduring friends with whom there is regular but infrequent contact was a reoccurring finding in the interviews. These enduring friendships do not neatly fit into the strong-tie/weak tie-dichotomy discussed in Chapter 3, because intimate connections with these friends occur infrequently over long stretches of time. Participants felt emotionally close to these friends, but not in the same way as the close friends that they connect with more actively.

Tricia described these types of friends as follows:

Like some of my friends, they're still my friends, but they're not the ones that I'm seeing all the time. But that doesn't mean that they're not good friends. It just means that because of their schedules or my schedule, where we live, you know, what's going on in our lives, maybe we just don't see each other the same amount as with my girlfriends.

Enduring friendships are a prime example of how relational complexity can occur in the context of voluntarily maintaining friendships. Unlike interaction that occurs through the roles that individuals maintain in work and family institutions; individuals must choose to stay in touch with friends. The frequency of connection varied from weekly to yearly. But common to respondents' descriptions of these ties was the fact that they are not close in the same ways as their very close friends that they see more frequently.

The interviews show that the ease with which individuals can connect with enduring friendships by way of technological means is critical to their existence. Natalie, a homemaker in her fifties, made this clear:

I guess I have a couple of friends that we don't really speak on the phone with. It's easier just to text "Happy Birthday" or "Merry Christmas" and, yeah there are a couple friends like that . . . you know they are old friends, but we don't see each other often. So, it's not the people that I kind of pick up the phone, [and say] "hey how are you doing." More of a, you know, "oh nice to hear from you" type of thing, for an occasion or something like that. We are just not in each other's lives on a daily basis, but we're still friends. Old friends, but we just don't communicate often.

Given that these long-tie relationships are often geographically distant, mediated communication is a necessary part of their existence. Without at least occasional calling or texting, these relationships would be completely dormant. As discussed in Chapter 3, in addition to voluntary calling and texting, social media platforms seem to play a role in helping individuals maintain these enduring friendships over time. Reading social media updates posted by these ties can help to maintain what Keith Hampton (2016) has termed *pervasive awareness.*

It is important to acknowledge that these ties have existed before constant connectivity, more often through occasional phone calls, letter writing, and later, email. The potential for constant connectivity, however, has enabled the possibility of reaching others in a greater variety of ways. Knowing that an old friend can be easily reached through a brief text or social media message (as opposed to sitting down to write an email or letter), and that such a message will reach them directly without interrupting their activities, lowers the barrier to maintaining enduring friendships. It also opens up the possibility of arranging ephemeral calling, video chat, or an in-person get-together.

In sum, this study shows how enduring relationships can be maintained over long periods of time through the practice of media situatedness and the maintenance of temporal boundaries. While it is beyond the scope of this study, these results suggest that these practices might help individuals foster a greater number of enduring friendships over the course of their lives, thereby adding further social complexity to personal networks.

SUPPORTIVE FRIENDSHIPS

Support is another dimension of friendship that is of critical importance to social life. As with the other types of ties, participants in this study were asked to think of one person that has helped them with something they considered to be important. About 50% of those completing the national survey considered these supportive ties to be very close, 15% considered them to be somewhat close, and the remaining respondents did not indicate that they had any level of closeness with these supportive ties.

Henry, a doctor in his mid-thirties, discussed a supportive friend that he met through mutual friends. This person helped him to find a roommate, and although he does not feel very close to him, he describes this friend as "Somewhat close. But close enough to trust his judgment." He texts this friend when "we are gonna go hiking or something, or going to the orchestra. Like if he is running late, we would call each other." Henry contacts this person about once every three weeks and occasionally views his posts on social media. Henry's relationship with this friend is clearly not strong, yet he draws on a combination of media to maintain regular but infrequent contact with him. Given their infrequent in-person contact, it seems unlikely that Henry would connect with this supportive relationship as frequently without the easy and direct connection of texting. Without constant connectivity and the ease of texting, it is unclear if these types of weaker supportive relationships would be maintained.

Although Henry's example shows how supportive ties are not necessarily strong, the survey results of this study show patterns of media use with supportive friends that are similar to those of very close friends. In the past week, 66% of the participants texted supportive friends, 58% saw them in-person, 46% called them, 25% read their social media posts, and 22% messaged them through a social media app. Participants connected with their supportive friends in the past week using an average of 2.3 media. The results of the logged analysis further show similarities between very close and supportive ties in terms of the frequency and regularity of calling and texting (see Table 9.2). For example, respondents report an average of 2.6 calls per 10-day period with their very close friends, and 2.0 with their somewhat close friends. Texting was even higher among supportive friends than very close friends, with an average of 37.6 versus 23.7 texts exchanged per 10-day period, respectively.

Mei's relationship with her supportive friend is an example that reflects the media patterns found in the survey and logged data. She met this friend through a previous job eight years ago and now lives a short walk away from her home. She sees this friend several times a week, and also contacts her using two social media apps. When asked why she uses one app over the other she explained,

> If I can't find her on WhatsApp, then I'll try to text her from WeChat. And when I try to call her, I'll first call her phone number, and if she doesn't pick up, I'll call through WhatsApp, if not then I'll try to call through WeChat . . . . And oh but um there's still times that she still doesn't pick up, then I'll have to call at her home, which I don't like we don't usually do, cuz it'd be her mum picking up the call [chuckles] yeah.

Mei knows when to text and when to call her friend because she is intimately aware of her friend's schedule. Her strategy of reaching her through various means shows that in the context of close relationships, this strategy is possible through the technological complexity that exists by having many communication apps and a variety of media functionality within apps. This example further shows how the potential for constant connectivity has created a situation in which supportive friends are constantly reachable, in this case by multiple apps on a single device.

In sum, respondents practice media situatedness as they draw on a variety of media to maintain contact with supportive friendships. They also show respect for temporal boundaries by using artifact-based media when their friends might be unavailable. These practices help them to actively maintain these supportive relationships.

POLITICALLY DIVERSE FRIENDSHIPS

Friendships with others that hold different beliefs constitute another important dimension of friendship. My work with Ken'ichi Ikeda (2011) has shown that interaction with these types of relationships has the potential to foster political deliberation. When these diverse ties are friends—rather than simply family members or work colleagues with whom individuals are forced to interact—there is even more potential for these relationships to facilitate productive political deliberations, as there is likely a stronger desire to consider alternative viewpoints. Nevertheless, while these relationships are voluntary and often involve some level of emotional connection, this study only shows that their influence on political deliberation is mixed.

In the surveys and interviews, participants were asked to think of one person they know who holds political views that are different from their own. Approximately 40% of the respondents considered these diverse ties to be friends. Communication with these diverse friend ties tends to involve fewer media than with the other friend ties examined in this chapter (see Table 9.1). In the previous week, respondents reported connecting with these ties using an average of 1.6 media. Thirty-seven percent of the respondents texted these ties, 32% saw them in-person, 27% messaged them using social media apps, 26% called them, and 25% read their social media posts. Compared to other friend ties, respondents also had less frequent and regular calling and texting with their diverse friends (see Table 9.2).

Moreen, a politically active librarian in her forties identifies such a tie as "my best friend for the past thirty-odd years. We met probably at a party when we were teenagers." Despite feeling close, she hasn't seen this friend since she moved to another province more than ten years ago. She messages this friend through Facebook messenger if there is "something that's going on in our personal lives. Sort of getting up to date on what the kids are doing."

Although they do not discuss political issues, she is aware of her friend's political views through her social media postings. In her words, her friend is "very deep into that wormhole of Trump and [the] rebel network. It's very sad." When asked if she ever considers disconnecting from this friend, she replies, "I have, but I feel keeping the connection is more likely to change their mind—to become more open about what they are currently very closed-minded about." She explains that she sometimes attempts to indirectly communicate with her through her family. "Sometimes there's indirect communication where I'll reach out to their family and ask 'Why are they posting this crap? What's going on?' And then they would reach out to her."

Moreen's relationship with her friend is an example of an enduring friend with whom communication has become entirely mediated. Their artifact-based exchanges through social media messaging and posts are the only means by which they maintain communication. On the one hand, Moreen's decision to stay connected to this person with the hope that her influence might help them to "become more open" shows that there is some attempt at facilitating political deliberation through social media. On the other hand, the fact that she is not comfortable directly engaging her friend on this topic does not provide much reason to believe that this will be a likely outcome.

Moreen practices media situatedness by choosing media that do not engage her directly in political conversations with her friend. While she does not state this directly, it is possible that her use of artifact-based media (messaging and posting) allows her to avoid direct conflict, rather than to simply maintain temporal boundaries.

In contrast to Moreen, other respondents are somewhat more blasé when discussing their communication with these types of diverse friends. In the words of Zander, a forensics video analyst in his forties, "It's different political views. But that's not what's framing the relationship. I don't think just because we have different views doesn't mean, like, I don't normally text them on a regular basis . . . . If that makes sense." For Zander, the political views of his friends are not a central part of his relationship, and as such they do not directly influence his media choices. He explains that he occasionally discusses politics with these types of friends, but these conversations are not very important to him.

In sum, these results show that respondents sometimes practice media situatedness when they select media that they feel will help them to avoid disagreements. This approach to media situatedness is similar to the approach that was discussed in the last chapter in the context of politically diverse family ties. Drawing on artifact-based media can help respondents maintain contact with these relationships while at the same time keeping an emotional distance. This has the effect of creating a division of media, where respondents tend to keep these diverse ties separate from their other relationships by mostly communicating with them through artifact-based media. While these results are somewhat supportive of the idea that communication media might play a role in maintaining diverse friendships, they do not suggest that this relational maintenance produces political deliberation.

CONCLUSION

This study shows that individuals reflexively draw on a range of media to stay connected to several types of friendships. I find that media situatedness is highly important to friendship because these relationships often require more active maintenance than institutionally based relationships. The specific medium that individuals choose in a given situation depends on several factors related to their knowledge of their friend's availability, the reason for the communication, and the nature of their connection more broadly. Temporal boundaries often factor into which media are selected, particularly in less close and enduring friendships, where individuals are less likely to know about their friends' availability. And finally, as individuals often connect to different sets of friends, a division of media naturally occurs through direct ephemeral and artifact-based exchanges.

The existence of enduring friendships also speaks to the importance of mediated communication practices in maintaining friendships over long periods of time. These relationships do not fit neatly into the strong-tie/weak tie-dichotomy, and mediated communication is a defining feature of their existence. While enduring friendships existed before the development of mobile devices, communication within these relationships now appears to be almost entirely mediated.

Overall, these results show how the active and reflexive use of many different communication options to connect with different kinds of friends has created a situation in which complex communication technology has become deeply embedded into complex friendship networks. In this way, practices of connection stem from and perpetuate social complexity in the context of friendship.

The Digital Bind

Constant connectivity alone has not changed social life. However, it has facilitated the emergence of new communication practices within the context of complex social and technological configurations. The practices of connection that I call media situatedness, the division of media, and temporal boundaries are all ways in which individuals leverage complex technological configurations in order to maintain complex personal networks. It is through these practices that the digital binds to the social.

In this concluding chapter, I will explore the various ways in which the practices of connection that I have identified through this study represent a digital bind at the intersection of constant connectivity, social configurations, and technological configurations. I will then discuss how these practices reconfigure social life, and close by considering possible long-term implications of the digital bind.

PRACTICES OF CONNECTION AND THE DIGITAL BIND

Through this empirical study, I have shown the various ways in which practices of connection situatedness stem from and perpetuate both social and technological complexity. In what ways do these digitally mediated practices bind us together?

The Digital Bind. Jeffrey Boase, Oxford University Press. © Oxford University Press (2025).
DOI: 10.1093/oso/9780197798591.003.0011

Media Situatedness

Media situatedness exists at the intersection of constant connectivity, complex social configurations, and complex technological configurations. If connectivity was not possible at any given moment, individuals would not as often be in situations where they need to consider the most appropriate communication option. Nor could they assume that their attempts to contact someone in their network would be successful. If personal network complexity did not exist in the form of actively and often voluntarily maintained social ties, individuals would have less reason to consider how they ought to connect with others because most interactions would be routine and habitual. If technological complexity did not exist, individuals would not have the many media options required to make a nuanced choice. Media situatedness exists in its current form because all of these "if conditions" are consistently satisfied for a large majority of the population.

Media situatedness represents a digital bind in that it has become the modus operandi of social life. The assumption of constant connectivity and the availability of complex media options are now so prevalent that they have become integral to how we relate to our complex personal networks of work, family, and friendship ties. If these digital systems were to disappear, social life could not exist in its current form. It is through the confluence of all these factors that media situatedness is possible, and it is through this practice of connection that the digital binds us together.

The Division of Media

The division of media is another practice of connection in which the digital binds with the social. When practicing media situatedness, individuals often enact strategies in which they primarily connect with certain individuals through particular media as a means of maintaining social separation. Other times, this division of media emerges organically as our existing social ties bring us into separate conversation threads and media channels. These practices reveal the complexity of social life as we are constantly moving between different sets of family, work, and friendship ties.

The division of media is possible due to the technological complexity that occurs when multiple communication options are available via communication apps. Moreover, constant connectivity helps to ensure that these options are viable means of connecting with a variety of social ties. Like media situatedness, the division of media exists in its current form through a combination of constant connectivity and complex social and technological configurations. It represents a binding of the digital and the social through the continued separation of relationships across various media.

Temporal Boundaries

The digital bind is also found in the practice of maintaining temporal boundaries. Without this practice, individuals would potentially face constant interruption as a result of constant connectivity. The ability to exchange digital artifacts through text, voice, and video messages provides options that enable individuals to navigate and avoid such a predicament. These options arise from technologically complex configurations. The need to maintain a flow of activities while simultaneously attending to multiple engagements is emblematic of schedule complexity, which is a key dimension of contemporary social life. Once again, we find a practice of connection that is predicated on the binding of constant connectivity, technological complexity, and social complexity.

Power and Practices of Connection

As I have theorized and shown through this study, power in the form of communicative autonomy flows through and potentially modifies these three practices. Tensions arise when workers lack the autonomy to fully practice media situatedness and enforce temporal boundaries. These tensions can also arise within family relationships, particularly in the case of children wishing to exercise autonomy from their parents. While I do not find much evidence of power influencing these practices within more voluntary, non-institutionally based friendships, it is conceivable that power manifests itself more subtly in these relationships.

When individuals have autonomy to freely choose how they use communication technology, it often fades into the background. When inequalities within relationships and institutions constrain and prevent us from freely engaging in our practices of connection, we feel technology's presence more viscerally.

COEVOLUTION AND RECONFIGURATION

In as much as the digital binds the social, the social also binds the digital. Recall from Chapter 2 that technology also has agency, in that it carries out the actions required for mediated communication to occur. Without this agency, mediated communication would not be possible. While it is tempting to think of technology as passively serving the human need for connection, humans also serve technology as they continue to maintain and develop it into ever–more technologically complex systems. It is in this way that human and technological actions coexist and coevolve through the development of new mediated communication practices. Through these practices of connection, the technological and the social become mutually embedded.

As practices of connection become widespread and repeated over time, they represent a new type of socio-technical configuration. The configuration approach draws on Anthony Giddens' theory of structuration, in which recurring actions (i.e., practices) continually recreate social structures (i.e., social configurations). It further extends this approach by considering the structuration that occurs as technologies act according to their own particular configurations. The practices of connection that I have uncovered through this study are social in that humans engage in them, yet at the same time they are technological, in that media technologies must also act. For example, if I send a text message to a friend, this obviously requires action on my part. At the same time, my phone, the connecting wireless communications systems, and my friend's phone must also act in order for this message to be sent. As human and technological actions are co-occurring and reoccurring over time through common practices of connection, a socio-technical configuration that is both social and technological emerges over time. In this way, common practices of connection represent emergent configurations that exist as a mutual binding of the digital and the social.

These emergent socio-technical configurations, in turn, reconfigure social life. While it is true that personal networks were complex before the development of these practices, it is important to recognize that these practices bring with them new social rules. For example, when an individual respects a friend's temporal boundaries by choosing to text rather than call, they are reflexively considering social rules about the various factors that are most salient to this decision. Before constant connectivity and the development of complex communication technologies, these rules did not exist because this type of situation could not exist. It is through the adoption of new social rules that stem from and perpetuate social complexity that social life is reconfigured.

POSSIBLE FUTURES

The embedding of the technological into the social has resulted in a situation in which the possibility of constant connectivity is now a precondition of social life. While it is still possible to carry out relationships without any form of digital mediation, these relationships have become extremely rare and impractical for most people. What are the long-term implications of this deep integration of the digital and the social?

While it is common to assume that the telecommunication infrastructures that enable the possibility of constant connectivity are robust and consistently available, this is not necessarily the case. On July 8, 2022, more than 12 million people in Canada lost cable and cellular service due to an unexpected telecommunications infrastructure disruption.

Although most services were restored by the next day, the fallout was enormous. Work and social life was thrown into disarray, creating public outrage (Rajagopal and Shakil 2022). In addition to these social and professional disruptions, emergency services were unavailable, as were basic debit and credit card transactions. In short, life for most of the country suddenly stopped. While there have since been improvements to this critical infrastructure, this episode shows the magnitude of disruption that is possible when communication services become unavailable in a digitally bound society.

As climate change increases the frequency and scope of natural disasters, the precariousness brought about by our collective digital bind will become more evident. In the short term, it is likely that economically developed countries will continue to improve their telecommunication infrastructures as a means of mitigating this precariousness. However, countries lacking the economic means of making these improvements will likely experience severe hardships. While the longer-term implications are less clear, it is worth considering that many of the components within mobile devices and networked infrastructure come from international supply chains. As natural disasters intensify, it is possible that these supply chains will be more consistently impacted and critical components of communication technologies will become scarce. Given that we have woven these technologies so deeply into our practices of connection, it is unclear how we will deal with this technological scarcity.

It is further worth considering the role of governments in ensuring the continued availability and use of communication technologies. As we have developed practices around the availability of multiple media options, governments that attempt to limit or control our access to these options will directly limit our ability to freely connect and communicate. The implications for free expression and association with others are concerning. Now that digital media are so deeply woven into social life, it is more critical that we make choices that protect and improve the availability and privacy of these complex, technologically networked configurations. Otherwise, the digital bind may prove to be too tight.

APPENDIX

The Promise and Perils of Digital Methods

Communication practices are a type of human behavior that can be difficult to study. Behavior happens constantly, and although we are aware of what we are doing at any one moment, we are not naturally disposed to recalling all of our actions in much detail, particularly over long periods of time. During a survey, interview, or informal conversation, it is possible to ask people to describe their communication practices, but these "self-reports" may not reflect reality. People might not wish to be truthful, perhaps because the reality of their actions does not align with how they see themselves or their social lives. They may simply not be able to recall previous interactions with much accuracy. However, at times, "self-report" approaches can be the only way of learning about communication practices, in which case researchers have developed options that can obtain better information. For example, in my work with Rich Ling, I found that certain survey questions about mobile phone use produced a more accurate understanding of how frequently people call or text than other questions (Boase and Ling 2013). However, these options often provide only a basic understanding of certain types of behaviors, which don't fully do justice to the nuance and complexity of behavior.

Another approach is to observe people if your goal is only to understand how a small number of people behave. But if you want to generalize to a larger set of people (perhaps an entire society), or if you want to know what people really do when they are not being observed, this approach is limited. There are ways of increasing confidence about the data obtained with this approach, such as when ethnographers spend time talking with and listening to how a community understands or makes sense of their own interactions. Ethnographic approaches can help to build a picture of behavior that provides insight into how people think about their behaviors. Nevertheless, generalizing these insights from a particular community to a larger population cannot always be done with certainty.

It is in the context of the limitations endemic to more traditional social science methods that digital methods—sometimes called "big data"—seem to hold so much promise. This type of data captures certain types of behavior in great detail without relying on human memory or self-reporting, meaning that it can be a much better reflection of actual behavior than more traditional interview or survey methods. Moreover, big data can potentially be collected from large sets of individuals, which enables the possibility of greater generalizability. At the same time, methods using big data are not without methodological and ethical problems. Before continuing, it is useful to consider what exactly is meant by "big data" and "digital methods."

David Lazer and Jason Radford (2017) classify big data into three types: digital life, digital trace, and digitized life. Digital life refers to aspects of daily life that occur by digital means, including most behaviors that occur on platforms like Twitter, Facebook, or Wikipedia. These types of behaviors have been woven into daily interactions and routines, and the data recording of these behaviors is often collected and owned by the platforms' companies. In contrast, digital traces are metadata that record actions taken through digital technology. For example, call detail records (CDRs) are automatically collected on mobile phones, by phone companies, and sometimes by companies that operate mobile software. They include information about the time and date of calls, the phone numbers making and receiving the calls, and call duration. CDRs are considered traces rather than digital life because they are records about only certain aspects of an action, rather than the action itself. Finally, Lazer and Radford defined digitized life as life that is not directly digital but nevertheless can be captured by digital means. Digitized life encompasses digital video recordings taken in public places, the digitization of previously analog books or news articles, and the inference of location based on the proximity of mobile devices to cell towers.

At this point, even a reader who is optimistic about the role that big data might play in understanding human behavior will no doubt see its potential perils. Most importantly, digital life, digital traces, and digitized life all produce data that may be collected without clear consent, or even awareness that they are being collected at all. While it may be true that platforms such as Twitter and Facebook require that individuals sign legal agreements to consent to data collection, it is well known that these agreements often contain difficult language, are extremely lengthy, and don't clearly communicate how and why data will be collected. Moreover, consent ought to be given freely, without pressure or coercion, making it difficult to ensure that individuals do not face social pressures by their friends and families to join these platforms. Finally, there are other ethical issues, such as how data is safeguarded to ensure privacy; sensitive data may be collected without any specific purpose, and data can be used inappropriately, leading to harm.

It may not be possible to overcome all ethical issues in many cases. For example, data may have already been collected by social media companies without voluntary informed consent. However, there are ways of addressing many of the ethical issues when designing a research study. As I have argued previously (Boase 2013), social researchers have been conducting studies in which they have dealt with sensitive and potentially compromising topics for decades. For example, ethnographers often find themselves in situations in which they learn sensitive and potentially compromising things about participants in the communities that they research. Researchers conducting surveys or in-depth interviews also sometimes learn sensitive information from their respondents that could damage them if made public.

To avoid harming respondents who participate in their studies, social researchers have developed ethical standards. First and foremost, informed consent is a standard that has been widely agreed upon as a basic requirement for nearly all research designs. Informed consent means that respondents should be clearly presented with information about how and why data is being collected. Such information should be freely given as participation is ongoing. If respondents change their minds, they can stop participating and have the option of removing their data

Appendix

(to the extent that it is possible). Researchers can promise not only confidentiality (i.e., that they will not reveal respondent's identities to others) but also anonymity. Social researchers have also developed ethical review boards, which exist in universities, in industries, and sometimes as independent organizations. These boards review proposals for new studies, providing researchers with insights regarding ethical issues that may not have been immediately apparent to them and ensuring that new studies meet shared ethical standards. Finally, social researchers have learned to only collect the data that they need and avoid collecting data that is not directly useful to them. All these approaches help to reduce the potential for harm.

Aside from ethical concerns, big data methodologies are not without limitations. Despite the great promise that these data will provide researchers, with previously unattainable insights into the detailed behavior of large sets of individuals, there is much that these data lack. In many cases, data are ultimately vast records of particular behaviors, and as such, they lack information about the context in which the behaviors occurred and what they actually mean to individuals. For example, a collection of "likes" on social media could include many millions of rows indicating the time, date, and account names of the individuals giving likes and those receiving the likes. However, this same vast dataset might be lacking information on which individuals clicked these likes, what they mean to those receiving them (or if those on the receiving end even noticed who gave them), and the social role of the individuals (are they "friends," colleagues, or distant relatives?). While this lack of context and meaning might not be a hindrance for all research projects, it certainly places limitations on the knowledge and insights that could be extracted from a large set of data.

Aside from lacking context and meaning, big data has other limitations, depending on the exact type of data and the situation in which it was collected. For example, social media data collected from sites such as Twitter can contain data generated by bots—scripts that carry out actions intended to trick others into believing that they are human. Another limitation occurs when coders who develop scripts for the collection of digital data introduce bugs or errors that produce data that do not reflect actual behavior. Sometimes there is simply too much data for researchers to be able to make sense of, because they lack either the computational power or approaches to analyze it. The promise of big data for providing a new source of information about human behavior is undeniable. Nevertheless, it is important to temper excitement about this new type of data with an understanding of the ethical and methodological issues it brings.

NOTES

CHAPTER 1

1. This review is similar in nature to reviews by mobile scholars Scott Campbell (2018, 2020) and Rowan Wilken (2009), although there is more focus here on the empirical findings that underlie the development of these terms.
2. Technically, texting was actually email in Japan. This is because telecommunication companies had incompatible SMS protocols, and as a result, short text-based messages were exchanged using email protocols instead (Ohta 2001). However, the opportunities and constraints for interaction provided by these short text-based email messages were the same as regular SMS text messages.

CHAPTER 2

1. Wanda J. Orlikowski (1992) also applied Giddens' structuration theory to technology within the context of formal organizations. The configuration approach applies structuration more broadly to understand the role that technology plays in a variety of formal and informal social contexts, including friendship, family, and various kinds of occupations. While it is similar to Orlikowski's approach in that it applies Giddens' structure/agency duality to technology, this broader focus beyond formal organizations allows for a more extensive set of considerations and applications.

CHAPTER 3

1. For example, throughout this work, Tönnies argues that preindustrial communities are based on "natural" relationships, particularly "the relation between husband and wife in its natural or general biological meaning" (p. 37). This highly problematic idea that what is "natural" can be used to classify various social relationships runs throughout Tönnies' discussion of community relationships.
2. For Merton, roles exist independently of the individuals that occupy them (Hage and Powers 1992). For example, the role of "nurse" is not determined by a particular individual who plays that role but, rather, by the set of explicit and implicit rights and obligations expected of anyone occupying that role. This definition then assumes the existence of fairly stable social institutions that have existed long enough for expectations surrounding roles to be clearly defined and

understood. In the context of late industrial societies, this was a reasonable assumption, and we will revisit it later when discussing the utility of this approach in contemporary society.

CHAPTER 4

1. Word processing allowed personal computers to play a role in letter writing, displacing the use of the typewriter. However, this role was limited to the production of letters, and the mail system remained the primary means of these types of exchanges. It is also worth noting that while a few individuals did use dial-up modems to connect directly to other computers that served as "bulletin boards" via landline phone connections, few computer users in the 1980s and 1990s engaged in this type of communication
2. Given that these systems were only accessible in website format, they were originally called social media sites rather than social media platforms.
3. The posting of videos (which involved audio) was limited when many social media platforms launched.
4. It should be noted that some governments severely restrict the number of communication apps available to citizens. For example, at present, China allows few communication apps except for WeChat. However, this level of restriction is uncommon in most countries.

CHAPTER 5

1. Eight respondents installed the app but did not complete the survey.
2. This response rate calculation compensated for the fact that for 0.01% of the invitations, the addresses no longer existed or contained errors.
3. Seventy-six percent of Canadians owned a smartphone in 2016 (Statistics Canada 2017). StatCounter (GlobalStats 2018) shows that in 2017, 51% of smartphones used iOS operating systems and 46% used the Android operating system. This means that the total percentage of Canadians with Android phones was roughly 35% at the time of this survey.
4. In this analysis, statistically significant differences are those with P values greater than 0.05.
5. This calculation is based on the Canadian population estimate of 28,533,553 adults in 2017 (Statistics Canada 2017).

CHAPTER 6

1. Mean = 8.3, median = 9, standard deviation (S.D.) = 2.7.
2. The media options provided to respondents in the surveys were as follows: In-person conversation, phone call, email, text message, social media direct message (Facebook Messenger, Snapchat, Instagram, and so on), reading posts on social media (Facebook, Twitter, and so on), video call (Skype, Hangouts video, and so on), online or console games (Ventrilo, Xbox live chat, and so on), other, or did not communicate with them in the past seven days.
3. It should be noted that to reduce the time and effort required to complete the surveys, instead of asking respondents to indicate all the possible social media they used to connect with particular relationships, they were instead asked to

Notes

indicate if they connected with them through social media direct messages or read their posts on social media. If they had been asked to indicate the specific social media used to message and read posts, it is quite reasonable to expect the total number of media combinations to be much higher than reported here.

4. Given that 80% of respondents reported using social media apps on their phone, the result that 5% have not used any social media apps in the past month implies that 15% of respondents use social media only on computers and not on their phones.

5. Mean = 3.0, median = 3, S.D. = 1.9.

6. I have advocated for this distinction between ephemeral and digital artifact media rather than the seemly parallel and more commonly used distinction between synchronous and asynchronous media because digital artifact media are not necessarily asynchronous. At times, individuals may be absorbed in artifact-based activities such as texting, such that the constant reading and respondent is nearly synchronous, even though the technology does not demand it be used in this way.

CHAPTER 7

1. The percentage of employed respondents reported here is slightly higher than the percentage reported in Chapter 5. This is because I used weighted data for my analysis here, while Chapter 5 uses unweighted data for comparative purposes.

2. To sort respondents into these occupational categories, I drew on survey questions from the project's national surveys, in which participants reported their job description and level of education. In these surveys we did not ask respondents to report their income, because it is well known among survey researchers that respondents rarely disclose this information with much accuracy, even in anonymous surveys such as this one. The job titles were used to infer the type of occupations in which respondents worked. There were twenty cases in which it was not possible to infer occupational type, and these cases are excluded from these results.

   Knowledge occupations include project management, accounting, IT management, and graphic design. Those working in service occupations include cleaners, cashiers, drivers, and shop caretakers. Public sector occupations include positions such as teachers, nurses, government bureaucrats, and those in the military. Goods production occupations include those working on factory floors, farmers, and construction workers.

3. To infer wage level, I used a combination of job title and education level.

CHAPTER 8

1. The survey did not ask respondents to report how many days a week these children lived in the same household. As such, it is difficult to know what portion of households with parents and children involved joint custody arrangements in which the children also lived in another household.

2. At first it may seem counterintuitive that these results differ somewhat between parents and children. However, all respondents in this study are adults, which means that the children in the same household tend to be nonadults. In other

words, the results relating to "children" are about the relationship between the adult parent and the nonadult child. In contrast, the results relating to "parents" are about the relationship between adult children living at home and their parents.

BIBLIOGRAPHY

Agar, Jon. 2003. *Constant Touch: A Global History of the Mobile Phone.* Cambridge, UK: Icon.

Archer, Margaret. 2012. *The Reflexive Imperative in Late Modernity.* Cambridge, UK: Cambridge University Press.

Arthur, W. Brian. 2009. *The Nature of Technology: What It Is and How It Evolves.* New York: Free Press.

Bayer, Joseph B., Sonya Dal Cin, Scott W. Campbell, and Elliot Panek. 2016. "Consciousness and Self-Regulation in Mobile Communication." *Human Communication Research* 42 (1): 71–97.

Beck, Ulrich. 1992. *Risk Society: Towards a New Modernity.* London: Sage Publications.

Beck, Ulrich, and Elizabeth Beck-Gernsheim. 2002. *Individualization.* London: Sage.

Bell, Daniel. 1973. *The Coming of Post-Industrial Society: A Venture in Social Forecasting.* Social Theory, 2nd ed. New York: Basic Books.

Bureau of Labor Statistics. 2020. "Employee Tenure in 2020." U.S Department of Labor. https://www.bls.gov/news.release/pdf/tenure.pdf.

Boase, Jeffrey. 2008. "Personal Network and the Personal Communication System." *Information, Communication and Society* 11 (4): 490–508.

Boase, Jeffrey. 2013. "Implications of Software-Based Mobile Media for Social Research." *Mobile Media & Communication* 1 (1): 57–62.

Boase, Jeffrey, John B Horrigan, and Barry Wellman. 2006. *The Strength of Internet Ties: The Internet and Email Aid Users in Maintaining Their Social Networks and Provide Pathways to Help When People Face Big Decisions.* Washington DC: Pew Internet and American Life Project.

Boase, Jeffrey, and Tetsuro Kobayashi. 2008. "Kei-Tying Teens: Using Mobile Phone e-Mail to Bond, Bridge, and Break with Social Ties: Aa Study of Japanese Adolescents." *International Journal of Human Computer Studies* 66 (12): 930–43.

Boase, Jeffrey, Tetsuro Kobayashi, Andrew Schrock, Tsutomu Suzuki, and Takahisa Suzuki. 2015. "Reconnecting Here and There: The Reactivation of Dormant Ties in the United States and Japan." *American Behavioral Scientist* 59 (8): 931–45.

Boase, Jeffrey, and Rich Ling. 2013. "Measuring Mobile Phone Use: Self-Report Versus Log Data." *Journal of Computer-Mediated Communication* 18 (4): 508–19.

Boase, Jeffrey, and Barry Wellman. 2006. "Personal Relationships: On and Off the Internet." In *The Cambridge Handbook of Personal Relationships*, edited by Dan Perlman and Anita L Vangelisti, 709–23. Oxford: Blackwell.

Boczkowski, Pablo J., Mora Matassi, and Eugenia Mitchelstein. 2018. "How Young Users Deal with Multiple Platforms: The Role of Meaning-Making in Social Media Repertoires." *Journal of Computer-Mediated Communication* 23 (5): 245–59.

Brewer, Devon. 2000. "Forgetting in the Recall-Based Elicitation of Personal and Social Networks." *Social Networks* 22: 29–43.

Brix, Andrew C. n.d. "Postal System." In Encyclopedia Britannica. Accessed September 7, 2022. https://www.britannica.com/topic/postal-system.

Bruno, Leonard C. 2004. "Telegraph." In *The Gale Encyclopedia of Science*, edited by K. Lee Lerner and Brenda Wilmoth Lerner, 3rd ed., 6:3970–72. Detroit, MI: Gale.

Bucher, Taina, and Anne Helmond. 2017. "The Affordances of Social Media Platforms." In *The SAGE Handbook of Social Media*, edited by Jean Burgess, Thomas Poell, and Alice Marwick, 233–53. London: SAGE Publications.

Burrell, Jenna. 2010. "Evaluating Shared Access: Social Equality and the Circulation of Mobile Phones in Rural Uganda." *Journal of Computer-Mediated Communication* 15 (2): 230–50.

Campbell, Scott W. 2018. "From Frontier to Field: Old and New Theoretical Directions in Mobile Communication Studies." *Communication Theory* 29 (1): 46–65.

Campbell, Scott W. 2020. "Cutting the Cord: Social and Scholarly Revolutions as CMC Goes Mobile." *Journal of Computer-Mediated Communication* 25 (1): 101–10.

Chen, Julie Yujie, and Ping Sun. 2020. "Temporal Arbitrage, Fragmented Rush, and Opportunistic Behaviors: The Labor Politics of Time in the Platform Economy." *New Media & Society* 22 (9): 1561–79.

Comer, Jonathan C., and Thomas A. Wikle. 2008. "Worldwide Diffusion of the Cellular Telephone, 1995–2005." *The Professional Geographer* 60 (2): 252–69.

Coser, Lewis A. 1974. *Greedy Institutions: Patterns of Undivided Commitment*. New York: Free Press.

Coser, Rose Laub. 1991. *In Defense of Modernity: Role Complexity and Individual Autonomy*. Stanford, CA: Stanford University Press.

Dimmick, John W. 2002. *Media Competition and Coexistence: The Theory of the Niche*. New York: Routledge.

Dimmick, John, Susan Kline, and Laura Stafford. 2000. "The Gratification Niches of Personal E-Mail and the Telephone: Competition, Displacement, and Complementarity." *Communication Research* 27 (2): 227–48.

Donner, Jonathan. 2007. "The Rules of Beeping: Exchanging Messages Via Intentional 'Missed Calls' on Mobile Phones." *Journal of Computer-Mediated Communication* 13 (1): 1–22.

Donner, Jonathan. 2008. "Research Approaches to Mobile Use in the Developing World: A Review of the Literature." *Information Society* 24 (3): 140–59.

Bibliography

Edwards, Jim. 2011. "The 10 Key Turning Points in the History of Social Media." *CBS News*, September 21, 2011, sec. Money Watch. https://www.cbsnews.com/news/the-10-key-turning-points-in-the-history-of-social-media/.

boyd, danah, and Nicole B. Ellison. 2007. "Social Network Sites: Definition, History, and Scholarship." *Journal of Computer-Mediated Communication* 13 (1): 210–30.

Erickson, Bonnie H. 2001. "Good Networks and Good Jobs: The Value of Social Capital to Employers and Employees." In *Social Capital: Theory and Research*, edited by Nan Lin, Karen Cook, and Ronald S. Burt, 127–58. Somerset, NJ: Taylor & Francis Group.

Fischer, Claude. 1992. *America Calling: A Social History of the Telephone to 1940*. Berkeley: University of California Press.

Fox, Jesse, and Bree McEwan. 2017. "Distinguishing Technologies for Social Interaction: The Perceived Social Affordances of Communication Channels Scale." *Communication Monographs* 84 (3): 298–318.

Gergen, Kenneth J. 2008. "Mobile Communication and the Transformation of the Democratic Process." In *Handbook of Mobile Communication Studies*, edited by James Katz, 297–310. Cambridge, MA: MIT Press.

Gibson, James. 1977. "The Theory of Affordances." In *Perceiving, Acting, and Knowing: Toward an Ecological Psychology*, edited by R. E. Shaw and J. Bransford, 67–82. Hillsdale, NJ: Lawrence Erlbaum Associates.

Giddens, Anthony. 1984. *The Constitution of Society*. Cambridge, UK: Polity Press.

GlobalStats. 2018. "Mobile Operating System Market Share in Canada: Jan - Dec 2017." http://gs.statcounter.com/os-market-share/mobile/canada/#monthly-201701-201712-bar.

Goggin, Gerard. 2021. *Apps: From Mobile Phones to Digital Lives*. Digital Media and Society Series. Cambridge, UK: Polity.

Goodman, David. 2005. "Linking Mobile Phone Ownership and Use to Social Capital in Rural South Africa and Tanzania." *Intermedia* 33 (4): 26–42.

Granovetter, Mark. 1973. "The Strength of Weak Ties." *American Journal of Sociology* 78 (6): 1360.

Granovetter, Mark. 1983. "The Strength of Weak Ties: A Network Theory Revisited." In *Social Structure and Network Analysis*, edited by Peter Marsden and Nan Lin, 105–30. Beverly Hills, CA: Sage.

Granovetter, Mark. 1995. *Getting a Job: A Study of Contacts and Careers*, 2nd ed. Chicago: University of Chicago Press.

Habuchi, Ichiyo. 2005. "Accelerating Reflexivity." In *Personal, Portable, Pedestrian: Mobile Phones in Japanese Life*, edited by Mizuko Ito, Misa Matsuda, and Daisuke Okabe, 165–82. MIT Press.

Hage, Jerald, and Charles H. Powers. 1992. *Post-Industrial Lives: Roles and Relationships in the 21st Century*. Thousand Oaks, CA: SAGE Publications.

Hampton, Keith N. 2016. "Persistent and Pervasive Community: New Communication Technologies and the Future of Community." *American Behavioral Scientist (Beverly Hills)* 60 (1): 101–24.

Haythornthwaite, Caroline. 2001. "Exploring Multiplexity: Social Network Structures in a Computer Supported Distance Learning Class." *Information Society* 17 (3): 211–26.

Haythornthwaite, Caroline. 2005. "Social Networks and Internet Connectivity Effects." *Information, Communication & Society* 8 (2): 125–47.

Hogan, Bernie. 2010. "The Presentation of Self in the Age of Social Media: Distinguishing Performances and Exhibitions Online." *Bulletin of Science, Technology & Society* 30 (6): 377–86.

Horst, Heather A., and Daniel Miller. 2006. *The Cell Phone: An Anthropology of Communication.* Oxford: Berg.

Humphreys, Lee. 2007. "Mobile Social Networks and Social Practice: A Case Study of Dodgeball." *Journal of Computer-Mediated Communication* 13 (1): 341–60.

Ikeda, Ken'ichi, and Jeffrey Boase. 2011. "Multiple Discussion Networks and Their Consequence for Political Participation." *Communication Research* 38 (5): 660–83.

Ito, Mizuko. 2005. "Mobile Phones, Japanese Youth, and the Re-Placement of Social Contact." In *Mobile Communications: Re-Negotiation of the Social Sphere*, edited by Rich Ling and Per E. Pedersen, 131–48. London: Springer.

Ito, Mizuko, Misa Matsuda, and Daisuke Okabe. 2005. "Portable, Personal, Pedestrian: Mobile Phones in Japanese Life." Cambridge, MA: MIT Press.

Kalev, Alexandra, and Gal Deutsch. 2018. "Gender Inequality and Workplace Organizations: Understanding Reproduction and Change." In *Handbook of the Sociology of Gender*, edited by Barbara J. Risman, Carissa M. Froyum, and William J. Scarborough, 257–69. Cham, Switzerland: Springer International.

Kane, Emily W., and Laura Sanchez. 1994. "Family Status and Criticism of Gender Inequality at Home and at Work." *Social Forces* 72 (4): 1079–102.

Katz, James E., and Mark A. Aakhus. 2002. *Perpetual Contact: Mobile Communication, Private Talk, Public Performance.* Cambridge, UK: Cambridge University Press.

Kobayashi, Tetsuro, and Jeffrey Boase. 2012. "No Such Effect? The Implications of Measurement Error in Self-Report Measures of Mobile Communication Use." *Communication Methods and Measures* 6 (2): 126–43.

Kobayashi, Tetsuro, and Jeffrey Boase. 2014. "Tele-Cocooning: Mobile Texting and Social Scope." *Journal of Computer-Mediated Communication* 19 (3): 681–94.

Kobayashi, Tetsuro, Jeffrey Boase, T. Suzuki, and T. Suzuki. 2015. "Emerging from the Cocoon? Revisiting the Tele-Cocooning Hypothesis in the Smartphone Era." *Journal of Computer-Mediated Communication* 20 (3): 330–45.

Latour, Bruno. 2004. "Nonhumans." In *Patterned Ground: Entanglements of Nature and Culture*, edited by Stephan Harrison, Steve Pile, and N. J. Thrift, 224–27. London: Reaktion Books.

Lazer, David, and Jason Radford. 2017. "Data Ex Machina: Introduction to Big Data." *Annual Review of Sociology* 43 (1): 19–39.

Licoppe, Christian. 2004. "'Connected' Presence: The Emergence of a New Repertoire for Managing Social Relationships in a Changing Communication Technoscape." *Environment and Planning D: Society and Space* 22 (1): 135–56.

Bibliography

Ling, Rich. 2008. *New Tech, New Ties: How Mobile Communications Is Reshaping Social Cohesion.* Cambridge, MA: MIT Press.

Ling, Rich. 2012. *Taken for Grantedness: The Embedding of Mobile Communication into Society.* MIT Press.

Ling, Rich, Johannes Bjelland, Pål Roe Sundsøy, and Scott W. Campbell. 2014. "Small Circles: Mobile Telephony and the Cultivation of the Private Sphere." *Information Society* 30 (4): 282–91.

Ling, Rich, Troels Fibæk Bertel, and Pål Roe Sundsøy. 2012. "The Socio-Demographics of Texting: An Analysis of Traffic Data." *New Media & Society* 14 (2): 281–98.

Ling, Rich, and Birgitte Yttri. 2002. "Hyper-Coordination via Mobile Phones in Norway." In *Perpetual Contact: Mobile Communication, Private Talk, Public Performance,* edited by Janes Katz and Mark Aakhus, 139–69. Cambridge: Cambridge University Press.

Marsden, Peter. 1987. "Core Discussion Networks of Americans." *American Sociological Review* 52 (1): 112–31.

Marsden, Peter, and Karen Campbell. 1984. "Measuring Tie Strength." *Social Forces* 62 (2): 482–501.

Milan, Anne. 2015. "The Shift to Smaller Households over the Past Century." Statistics Canada. Accessed December 16, 2021. https://www150.statcan.gc.ca/n1/pub/11-630-x/11-630-x2015008-eng.htm#def2.

Mumford, Lewis. 2010. *Technics and Civilization.* Chicago: University of Chicago Press.

Nagy, Peter, and Gina Neff. 2015. "Imagined Affordance: Reconstructing a Keyword for Communication Theory." *Social Media + Society* 1 (2): 205630511560338.

Norman, Donald A. 2013. *The Design of Everyday Things.* Rev. ed. New York: Basic Books.

Notopoulos, Katie. 2022. "Is Dead May Never Die: The Poke Feature Is Hidden, but It Can Be Uncovered." BuzzFeed News. November 30, 2022. https://www.buzzfeednews.com/article/katienotopoulos/facebook-poke-someone-today?utm_source=dynamic&utm_campaign=bfsharecopy.

Ohta, Hiroshi. 2001. "Mail No J-PHONE Tanjo Hiwa (The Secret of the Birth of J-PHONE Mail)." *Bessatsu Takarajima Real No. 014.* Takarajimasha.

Okada, Tomoyuki. 2005. "Youth Culture and the Shaping of Japanese Mobile Media: Personalization and the Keitai Internet as Multimedia." In *Personal, Portable, Pedestrian: Mobile Phones in Japanese Life,* edited by Mizuko Ito, Daisuke Okabe, and Misa Matsuda, 41–60. Cambridge, MA: MIT Press.

Onoda, Ryosuke, and Yasuhiro Omi. 2023. "The Value of Extracurricular Activities to Japanese Junior High School Students: Focusing on the Expression of a School's Attractiveness in Writing." *Frontiers in Education* 8: 1–6.

Orlikowski, W. J. 1992. "The Duality of Technology: Rethinking the Concept of Technology in Organizations." *Organization Science* 3 (3): 398–427.

Pertierra, Raul. 2008. "Technologies of Transformation: The End of the Social or the Birth of the Cyber Network?" In *Living the Information Society in Asia*, edited by Erwin Alampay, 36–56. Singapore: Institute of Southeast Asian Studies (ISEAS).

Pew Research Center. 2015. "Parenting in America: Outlook, Worries, Aspirations Are Strongly Linked to Financial Situation." Pew Research Center. https://www.pewresearch.org/social-trends/2015/12/17/1-the-american-family-today/.

PR Newswire. 2021. "50 Years of Email: But If the History of Email Tells Us Anything, It's That Email Isn't Going Away Any Time Soon." April 6. 2508794707. ABI/INFORM Collection; Global Newsstream. http://myaccess.library.utoronto.ca/login?qurl=https%3A%2F%2Fwww.proquest.com%2Fwire-feeds%2F50-years-email%2Fdocview%2F2508794707%2Fse-2%3Faccountid%3D14771.

Rajagopal, Divya, and Ismail Shakil. 2022. "Rogers Network Resuming after Major Outage Hits Millions of Canadians." Reuters. July 8. https://www.reuters.com/business/media-telecom/rogers-communications-services-down-thousands-users-downdetector-2022-07-08/.

Ramirez, Artemio, John Dimmick, John Feaster, and Shu-Fang Lin. 2008. "Revisiting Interpersonal Media Competition: The Gratification Niches of Instant Messaging, E-Mail, and the Telephone." *Communication Research* 35 (4): 529–47.

Sayes, Edwin. 2014. "Actor-Network Theory and Methodology: Just What Does It Mean to Say That Nonhumans Have Agency?" *Social Studies of Science* 44 (1): 134–49.

Schrock, Andrew Richard. 2015. "Communicative Affordances of Mobile Media: Portability, Availability, Locatability, and Multimediality." *International Journal of Communication* 9 (1): 1229–46.

Sharma, Sarah. 2014. *In the Meantime: Temporality and Cultural Politics*. Durham, NC: Duke University Press.

Statista. 2023. "Mobile Internet Usage Worldwide: Statistics & Facts." Statista. https://www.statista.com/topics/779/mobile-internet/#topicOverview.

Statistics Canada. 2017a. "Life in the Fast Lane: How Are Canadians Managing?" Statistics Canada. http://www.statcan.gc.ca/daily-quotidien/171114/dq171114a-eng.htm.

Statistics Canada. 2017b. "Population Estimates." Statistics Canada. http://www.statcan.gc.ca/tables-tableaux/sum-som/l01/cst01/demo02a-eng.htm.

Statistics Canada. 2021. "Study: A 30-Year Look at the Work Histories of Canadian Workers." Statistics Canada. https://www150.statcan.gc.ca/n1/daily-quotidien/211209/dq211209e-eng.htm#shr-pg0.

Stokols, Daniel. 1996. "Translating Social Ecological Theory into Guidelines for Community Health Promotion." *American Journal of Health Promotion* 10 (4): 282–98.

Suchman, Lucy. 2006. *Human-Machine Reconfigurations: Plans and Situated Actions*, 2nd ed. Learning in Doing: Social, Cognitive and Computational Perspectives. Cambridge: Cambridge University Press.

Sutko, Daniel, and Adriana de Souza e Silva. 2011. "Location-Aware Mobile Media and Urban Sociability." *New Media & Society* 13 (5): 807–23.

Thornton, A. 1989. "Changing Attitudes toward Family Issues in the United States." *Journal of Marriage and Family* 51 (4): 873–93.

Thornton, Arland, and Linda Young-DeMarco. 2001. "Four Decades of Trends in Attitudes toward Family Issues in the United States: The 1960s through the 1990s." *Journal of Marriage and Family* 63 (4): 1009–37.

Tönnies, Ferdinand. 1957. *Community & Society (Gemeinschaft Und Gesellschaft)*. East Lansing: Michigan State University Press.

Vanorman, Alicia, and Linda Jacobsen. 2020. "US Household Composition Shifts as the Population Grows Older; More Young Adults Live with Parents." Population Reference Bureau. https://www.prb.org/us-household-composition-shifts-as-thepopulation-grows-older-more-young-adults-live-with-parents/.

Vaughan, Theresa M., William J. Heetderks, Leonard J. Trejo, William Z. Rymer, Michael Weinrich, Melody M. Moore, Andrea Kübler, et al. 2003. "Brain-Computer Interface Technology: A Review of the Second International Meeting." *IEEE Transactions on Neural Systems and Rehabilitation Engineering* 11 (2): 94–109.

Wajcman, Judy. 2015. *Pressed for Time: The Acceleration of Life in Digital Capitalism*. Chicago: University of Chicago Press.

Wikipedia. n.d. "Timeline of Social Media." Wikipedia. Accessed September 9, 2022. https://en.wikipedia.org/wiki/Timeline_of_social_media.

Wilken, Rowan. 2009. "Bonds and Bridges: Mobile Phone Use and Social Capital Debates." In *Mobile Communication: Bringing Us Together and Tearing Us Apart*, edited by Rich Ling and Scott W. Campbell, 127–49. New Brunswick, NJ: Transaction.

Wu, Zheng, and Christoph M. Schimmele. 2011. "Changing Canadian Families." In *The Changing Canadian Population*, edited by Barry Edmonston and Eric Fong, 235–52. Montreal: McGill-Queen's University Press.

Zerubavel, Eviatar. 1985. *Hidden Rhythms: Schedules and Calendars in Social Life*. Berkeley: University of California Press.

Zhao, Xuan, Cliff Lampe, and Nicole B. Ellison. 2016. "The Social Media Ecology: User Perceptions, Strategies and Challenges." In *Proceedings of the 2016 CHI Conference on Human Factors in Computing Systems*, 89–100. CHI '16. New York: Association for Computing Machinery.

INDEX

For the benefit of digital users, indexed terms that span two pages (e.g., 52–53) may, on occasion, appear on only one of those pages.

Tables, figures, and boxes are indicated by an italic *t*, *f*, or *b*.

affordance, 25–29, 43–44
Archer, M, 34–36
artifact-based media, 84–85, 86*t*
    family, 155, 168–169
    friendship, 179, 181–182
    temporal boundaries, 126–129
    variety of communication options
      within apps, 87
    work, 138, 144, 146, 148, 150
asynchronous media, *see*
    ephemeral-based media
autonomy, *see* power

Beck, U, 12, 56–59, 64
Bell, D, 55–56
bounded solidarity, 11–12

calling, *see* ephemeral-based media
Campbell, S, 14
Canada
    demographics, 107*t*
    family arrangements, 154
    occupation type, 135
    personal network complexity, 102
coevolution, 187–188
common practices of connection, *see*
    practices of connection
complexity, *see* social complexity;
    technological complexity

configuration approach, 33–42, *see
also* affordance; social ecology;
    coevolution, mobile studies
'connected' presence, 13
constant connectivity, 1–2, 22–23
    common practices of connec-
      tion, 113–115, 125, 132–133,
      185–186
    communicative power, 129–130
    configuration approach, 47, 130–131
    early mobile studies, 16
    family, 163, 169
    friends, 177–179
    smartphones, 18–19, 47
    social complexity, 73, 115–118
    technological complexity, 81,
      115–118
    work, 140–141, 148, 150–152
Coser, R, 53–55, 59, 60, 62, 64–66,
    68–72

data collection app, 97–101
digital bind, 184–187, 189
digital trace data, 95–101, 105–106, 110
division of media, 114, 121–125, 116*f*
    complexity, social and
      technological, 131–132
    temporal boundaries, 127

economically disadvantaged
    countries, 17–18

Index

email, 31–32, 65, 77–80, 86*t*, 117*t*, 118,
    see also artifact-based media
ephemeral-based media, 84–85, 86*t*
  autonomy, 129
  family, 155, 160–161, 165
  friendship, 177, 182
  temporal boundaries, 114, 126–129,
    132
  variety of communication options
    within apps, 87
  work, 138, 145–146, 150
ethics in research, 97, 110
evolution, *see* coevolution

Facebook, *see* social media
family, *see also* artifact-based media;
    Canada; constant connectivity;
    ephemeral-based media; media
    situatedness; power; reflexivity;
    temporal boundaries
  children and parents, 161–164
  partners and spouses, 155–161
  politically diverse family, 167–168
  supportive family, 164–166
Fischer, C, 76
friendship, *see also* artifact-based media;
    constant connectivity; ephemeral-
    based media; media situatedness;
    power; reflexivity; technological
    complexity; temporal boundaries
  close, 171–176
  enduring, 176–177
  politically diverse, 180–182
  supportive, 178–179

generalization in research, 102–109
Giddens, A, 33–35, 72, 187–188
Granovetter, M, 15, 62–63

Humphreys, L, 20–21
hypercoordination, 13

individualization, 56–59, 64, 81
Instagram, *see* social media
internet, 77–81

Japan, 16–17

knowledge economy, 57

Ling, R, 11–12, 29–33, 43
locative services, 20–21

media multiplexity, 119–120
media situatedness, 114, 119–121, 116*f*,
    127, 131–132
  complexity, social and
    technological, 131
  digital bind, 185–186
  factors, 119
  family, 162–163, 166, 169
  friendship, 181–182
  work, 141, 146, 151
methods, *see* data collection app;
    sampling method
microcoordination, 13
mobile phone, 1–3, *see also* constant
    connectivity; bounded solidarity;
    'connected' presence; hyperco-
    ordination; monadic clusters;
    tele-cocooning
  activities, 117–118
  bonding, 9–15
  history, 81–82
  studies, 9–18, 20–21, 116*f*
monadic clusters, 11
multimethod research, 95–97

occupation
  autonomy, 50, 69–70, 129–130,
    136–138, 148–150, 152
  goods producing, 148–150
  knowledge, 136–144
  personal network complexity, 57,
    135–136, 151
  public sector, 147–148
  service, 144–147
  wage, 135

personal computers, 77–81
personal network complexity, *see* social
    complexity
platform labour, 71–72
power, 129–130, 132, 186–187
  communicative autonomy, 115

family, 164, 169
friendship, 186–187
personal network complexity, 68–72
role conflict, 68–71
work, 134, 149, 151–152
practices of connection, 38–39, 47–48,
39*t*, 49, 95, 113–115, 116*f*, 131, *see
also* constant connectivity; division
of media; temporal boundaries

reflexivity, 34–37
configuration approach, 38, 39*t*,
43–44, 47–48
family, 153, 168–169
friendship, 182–183
habit, 35–37, 185
individualization, 58–59
media situatedness, 116*f*, 120, 131
qualitative research, 109–111
relational complexity, 64–65, 116*f*
work, 138, 140, 142, 145, 146, 151

sampling method, 102–109
selective sociality, 10
service economy, 57
Sharma, S, 66–67
structuration theory, 33–35, 38, 72,
187–188
smartphones, 18–21, 46, 82, *see also*
constant connectivity
internet connection, 18–19
postsmartphone era, 82–83
technological complexity, 90,
115–117
social complexity
configuration approach, 72–73
dimensions, 59–67
industrial revolution, 51–52
institutional complexity, 60–62
personal networks, 55–59
relational complexity, 62–65
role complexity, 53–54
role conflict, 59, 61–62, 64, 68
temporal complexity, 65–67
SnapChapt, *see* social media
social affordance, *see* affordance

social ecology, 29–33, 42, 187–188
social media, 19–20, 79–80, 117*t*,
122–123
algorithms, 26, 37
apps, 2–3, 18–19, 86*t*
digital methods, 100–101, 106–107
division of media, 114, 121–125
messaging, 20–21
privacy, 130
de Souza e Silva, A, 20–21
strong ties, 11–12, 15, 16
synchronous media, *see*
ephemeral-based media

technological complexity, *see also*
constant connectivity
changing nature of apps and
devices, 87–89
configuration approach, 89–90
historic development, 74–77
friendship, 179
multiple communication apps, 115,
118
practices of connection,
common, 118, 123–124, 131
variety of communication options
within apps, 87
work, 142, 148, 151, 169
technological determinism, 3, 27
tele-cocooning, 10–11
telephone, landline, 76–77
texting, 26–29, *see also* artifact-based
media
temporal boundaries, 114–115, 116*f*,
125–129
complexity, social and
technological, 132
digital bind, 186–187
family, 158, 160–161, 164, 165–166,
169
friendship, 173–175, 177, 179, 181,
182
reflexivity, 128
work, 140, 144, 145–146, 148,
150–152

Index

tie strength, 51–64, *see also* weak ties; strong ties

Twitter, *see* social media

Wajcman, J, 65–66

WhatsApp, 101, *see also* social media

weak ties, 15, 20–21, 62–65

work, *see* artifact-based media; Canada; constant connectivity; ephemeral-based media; media situatedness; power; reflexivity; technological complexity; temporal boundaries

zero-sum perspective, 14–15

Zoom, 86*t*, *see also* ephemeral-based media

The manufacturer's authorised representative in the EU for product safety is Oxford
University Press España S.A. of El Parque Empresarial San Fernando de Henares,
Avenida de Castilla, 2 – 28830 Madrid (www.oup.es/en or product.safety@oup.com).
OUP España S.A. also acts as importer into Spain of products made by the manufacturer.

Printed in the USA/Agawam, MA
August 1, 2025

891350.005